CHINESE COOKING FOR BEGINNERS

THE ETHNIC KITCHEN

CHINESE COOKING FOR BEGINNERS

MORE THAN 65 RECIPES FOR THE EAGER COOK

HELENE SIEGEL

ILLUSTRATIONS BY YAN NASCIMBENE

HarperCollins*Publishers*

HarperCollins books may be purchased for
educational, business, or sales promotional use.
For information, please call or write: Special
Markets Department, HarperCollins Publishers,
Inc., 10 East 53rd Street, New York, NY 10022.
Telephone: (212) 207-7528; Fax: (212) 207-7222.

FIRST EDITION

Designed by Stephanie Tevonian

Library of Congress Cataloging-in-Publication Data

Siegel, Helene.
   Chinese cooking for beginners : More than 65
recipes for the eager cook / Helene Siegel.—1st ed.
       p.   cm.   —(The Ethnic kitchen)
   Includes bibliographical references and index.
   ISBN 0-06-016428-X
   1. Cookery, Chinese.   I. Title.   II. Series:
Siegel, Helene. Ethnic kitchen.
TX724.5.C5S575   1992   91-58384
641.5951—dc20

92 93 94 95 96 DT/RRD 10 9 8 7 6 5 4 3 2 1

To my son Joey, with love

CONTENTS

Many thanks to cooking teacher, cookbook author, and friend Hugh Carpenter for his invaluable help in setting this book on its proper course.

Thanks also to Betty Kim Lew for generously sharing what she knows by instinct, and to Kim Upton for passing along what she was taught. I am lucky to have such good friends.

HOW TO COOK
CHINESE FOOD

"If there is anything the Chinese are serious about, it is neither religion nor learning, but food," said the 20th-century artist and writer Lin Yutang.

The Chinese have been thinking and writing about the best way to feed themselves since the 10th century. A few well-defined principles have emerged:

Good eating depends upon quality ingredients. Since the ultimate goal of fine cooking is to reveal the sweet, unadorned, natural flavor of foods, you must start with the best, freshest ingredients. How fresh is fresh? In China, some seafood is cooked while still alive. Very fresh!

Economy is the unifying principle of Chinese home cooking. From the use of equipment and fuel to speed of preparation and cost of ingredients, this cuisine does not break the bank. Everyday cooking is based on grains and vegetables, with meat or seafood used sparingly, almost as condiments. The meats that are used—primarily pork and chicken—are inexpensive and the lesser cuts, like pork butt and chicken wings, are prized over less tasty, leaner cuts. Very little beef, no veal, imported cheeses, or expensive spices are called for. Leftover bits and pieces can always be used in delicious fried rice and noodle dishes. Good health is an added benefit of this naturally low-fat, high-carbohydrate diet.

Subtlety and balance are the goals of fine cooking. Just as other ethnic cuisines grew heavier and less refined in the United States, so has Chinese. Ironically, Cantonese cuisine—the most popular style featured in Chinese-American restaurants—is known throughout China as the most subtle and delicate. Here it is often misrepresented by overly sauced and sweetened foods.

SECOND ONLY TO FLAVOR IS TEXTURE. THE GREATEST DELICACIES, LIKE BIRD'S NEST, SHARK'S FIN, AND SEA CUCUMBER, ARE EXAMPLES OF PURE TEXTURE FOODS. IN EVERYDAY HOME COOKING, CERTAIN FOODS MAY BE USED PRIMARILY FOR TEXTURE. WATER CHESTNUTS, BAMBOO SHOOTS, ICEBERG LETTUCE, CUCUMBERS, AND FRIED WON TONS ADD CRUNCH, WHILE TOFU, BEAN THREADS, AND CERTAIN DRIED MUSHROOMS ARE ABSORBERS AND CARRIERS OF OTHER FLAVORS. AN INTERESTING DISH CONTAINS CONTRASTING TEXTURES, AND MEALS ARE DESIGNED TO BE MEDLEYS OF CONTRASTING TEXTURES, TEMPERATURES, AND TASTES.

THESE UNDERLYING PRINCIPLES DO NOT CONVEY THE LOVE AND APPRECIATION THE CHINESE HAVE FOR THEIR FOOD AND THE IMPORTANCE ATTACHED TO EATING WELL. THIS CUISINE OF RARE DELICACY AND RUSTIC SIMPLICITY HAS SUSTAINED A CULTURE FOR OVER 2000 YEARS AND HAS TRAVELED WELL ALL OVER THE WORLD. IN CHINA, ANOTHER WAY TO SAY HELLO IS, "HAVE YOU EATEN?"—A QUESTION NEVER TO BE TAKEN LIGHTLY.

.   .   .   .

"IF YOU LIKE GOOD FOOD, COOK IT YOURSELF," ADVISED LI LIWENG, A 17TH-CENTURY CHINESE POET AND PHILOSOPHER.

IF YOU HAVE DONE MUCH EATING IN GOOD CHINESE RESTAURANTS IN THE UNITED STATES, YOU ARE NOT SO FAR FROM RE-CREATING AUTHENTIC CHINESE FLAVORS IN YOUR OWN HOME. ACCORDING TO THE CHINESE, THE FIRST PREREQUISITE OF COOKING WELL IS EATING WELL. YOU HAVE PROBABLY BEEN RESEARCHING THIS SUBJECT UNKNOWINGLY FOR YEARS!

TWO THOUGHTS BEFORE MOVING INTO THE KITCHEN: A WELL-STOCKED PANTRY OF ASIAN SPECIALTY ITEMS IS KEY TO ENJOYING CHINESE COOKING. IMAGINE WHAT A PAIN IT WOULD BE TO HAVE TO RUN TO THE STORE FOR EGGS, BUTTER, OR MILK EVERY TIME YOU GOT THE URGE TO COOK AMERICAN

FOOD. WITH A FEW INEXPENSIVE ITEMS ON HAND, IT WILL BE POSSIBLE TO PREPARE CHINESE DISHES WITH NO MORE PREPLANNING THAN YOU DO WITH OTHER FOODS.

BECAUSE THIS STYLE OF COOKING AND EATING IS SO UNFAMILIAR TO MOST WESTERNERS, I RECOMMEND COOKING CHINESE FOOD ON AN OCCASIONAL BASIS, AND BUILDING UP SLOWLY TO AN ENTIRE CHINESE MEAL. SINCE SO MANY CHINESE DISHES COMBINE MEAT AND VEGETABLES, ONE STIR-FRIED DISH SERVED WITH RICE CAN MAKE A WONDERFUL WEEKNIGHT DINNER FOR MOST FAMILIES WITHOUT ANY EXTRA EFFORT.

A FEW TECHNIQUES
FOR THE NOVICE

STIR-FRYING is the most frequently used technique in the Chinese kitchen. Although it is possible to stir-fry in a skillet, it makes sense to invest in a wok if you plan on doing much Chinese cooking, since it is perfectly designed for that job.

It is essential to read the recipe through and prepare the ingredients prior to cooking. Once you turn on the heat and begin stir-frying, there's no time to run back and forth to the cutting board. Make sure all your ingredients, including such seasonings as garlic and ginger, are chopped and placed in piles on plates near the stove. Liquid sauce ingredients and the cornstarch mixture should be mixed in advance and ready nearby. I find it helpful to keep a platter or two within arm's reach and a good large spoon for stirring.

The good news is that all stir-fries follow pretty much the same order. Although you may need to rely on the recipes at first, eventually a logical pattern will emerge.

First place the dry wok over high heat. When it is good and hot, in about 2 minutes, add the oil by pouring it in a circle near the rim so that it drips down and coats the sides and bottom. Swirl the pan once or twice to be sure it is well coated. The oil will heat immediately.

Now it is time to add the ingredients. As they are being added, everything must be constantly stirred to ensure even cooking. Usually main ingredients like meat or seafood are added first, and then removed from the pan to avoid overcooking. Next come the seasonings, followed by vegetables, sauce, and the cooked meat. A mixture of cornstarch and water is added last to thicken the sauce. All stir-fried dishes taste best brought to the table immediately.

One difference between Chinese- and European-style cooking is that stir-frying is done over constant high heat. If food is burning or you have lost your place in the recipe, remove the wok from the heat rather than lower the flame. This is especially true of stir-frying on an electric range.

The cooking times are meant to guide you. With practice you will learn the aroma of ginger and garlic as heat releases their flavor, the bright color of perfectly stir-fried vegetables, and the look of a sauce that has remained on the heat too long. Just remember, stir-frying moves to a steady quick beat.

MARINATION for stir-fry dishes is short. Most poultry, pork, and seafoods need no more than 30 minutes' marination, or the time it takes to prepare the other ingredients. Beef is the only ingredient that calls for longer tenderizing. In Chinese marinades, egg white and cornstarch are used to coat foods, while soy sauce, dry sherry, and spices add flavor.

CHOPPING AND SLICING vegetables and meat for stir-fry recipes require that you follow this general principle: All ingredients should be cut uniformly to ensure even cooking—either thinly sliced, cubed, diced, or cut into matchsticks or julienned. As you gain more experience, you may want to combine contrasting shapes, like cubed chicken with thinly sliced vegetables, for greater visual interest. Chinese cooking calls for much more knife work than European; however it also calls for less cooking time. With practice and a good utensil, your chopping will pick up speed.

DEEP-FRYING, a popular Chinese technique, is off-putting for many Americans because of the amount of oil that must be used. However, there is no better way to fry battered foods quickly and crisply or to make delicious, crisp won tons and rice sticks. If you deep-fry properly, most of the oil will remain in the pan; only a small amount will be absorbed by the food.

Use a deep, sturdy pot or wok and do not reduce the amount of oil in the recipe, as it is the minimum necessary to coat the food properly. Using less oil will make frying more difficult, and accidents more likely to occur. Always test the oil, either with a thermometer made for that purpose or by dropping in a morsel of the food to be fried. If the oil is hot enough, bubbles will form around the food and it will rise to the top, turning golden and then brown. If food immediately browns or blackens, the heat needs to be reduced and tested again before proceeding. Deep-fried foods should always be drained, blotted with paper towels, and served immediately. Cooking oil may be cooled, strained, and reused once or twice.

STEAMING is a technique at which the Chinese are masters. All kinds of ingredients are steamed, from fish and sausages to vegetables and rice. If you are using a wok, place a rack made for that purpose in the wok and then fill the wok with water to within 1 inch of the rack. Seasonings like ginger or scallions may be added to the water for flavor. Bring the water to a boil, place the food on a plate on the rack, and reduce heat to a simmer. Cover and cook for the length of time called for in the recipe. Follow the same technique if you are using a steamer.

TO THICKEN A SAUCE WITH CORNSTARCH, the thickening

agent for all Chinese sauces, combine the cornstarch with an equal amount of cold water, or more water for a thinner sauce, in a small bowl. After the sauce has been added to the wok, bring it to a boil and then stir the cornstarch paste with a finger to recombine. Slowly drizzle in the paste, stirring constantly until the sauce thickens slightly and coats the food. You needn't add the entire mixture, just enough to lightly thicken the sauce. Immediately remove from heat to avoid overthickening.

To Peel and Devein Shrimp, pull the shell off with your fingers and discard. The intestinal vein runs along the back, not the inside curve, of the shrimp. Cut a ¼-inch slice along the center of the back with a paring knife. Remove the vein and rinse shrimp in cold water to remove any dirt.

To Fry Rice Sticks, bring about 2 cups peanut or corn oil to deep-fry temperature in a wok or medium skillet. Break the sticks into small batches and cook until white and puffy, about 10 seconds. Turn with tongs and cook an additional second until the sizzling stops. Drain on paper towels.

HOW TO SHOP FOR CHINESE COOKING

While most of the vegetables and seasonings necessary for cooking Chinese dishes are now available at well-stocked supermarkets, for the more esoteric bottled sauce ingredients and condiments it is worth a trip to a specialty market or Chinatown, if at all possible. Not only is it fun to rub shoulders with giant geoduck clams and thousand-year-old eggs, you will be amazed at how low the prices are for the very best ingredients. Even if you become an aficionado and cook Chinese fare regularly, you won't need to stock up on the basics more than twice a year.

INGREDIENTS

Note: An asterisk preceding an ingredient indicates an item recommended for daily cooking.

GRAINS AND STARCHES

*LONG-GRAIN RICE is the perfect accompaniment to most stir-fried dishes. In southern China, rice is the main course and meat and vegetable dishes are viewed as side dishes. Most of the rice sold in supermarkets is long grain, as is the rice available in bulk at Chinese markets—where a chalkboard may indicate the varieties and prices of rice in stock. Rice can be stored indefinitely in a well-sealed container at room temperature.

*EGG AND WHEAT NOODLES, invented by the Chinese, are staples of the northern Chinese diet. Although noodles for chow mein and lo mein are available fresh in Chinese specialty shops, the dried variety is easier to work with and tastes just as good. They are sold in some supermarkets in the Chinese section in 1-pound plastic bags labeled "Chinese-style egg-flavored noodles" or in 5-pound boxes at the Chinese market. Italian spaghettini is a good substitute. Like all dry pasta, Chinese noodles may be stored indefinitely.

*BEAN THREADS, also known as vermicelli, transparent, glass, or cellophane noodles, are made from ground mung bean starch and water. Although they can be deep-fried, they are more commonly softened in hot tap water for 15 minutes, drained, and then added to soups, stir-fries, and stuffings. While their taste is quite bland, they are excellent absorbers and carriers of other flavors. Available in Chinese markets, they are packaged in 1-pound bags or convenient packages of eight individual 1.8-ounce portions. They may be stored indefinitely at room temperature. Rice sticks or shredded lettuce may be substituted.

*RICE STICKS are the white dried noodles made of rice and water that grow puffy and crisp when deep-fried (see page 7 for technique). They are an important ingredient in Chinese salads and can be used as a crisp bed for stir-fry dishes. They may also be soaked and added to soups and stir-fries like bean threads. Sold in the Chinese section of supermarkets and specialty markets, a 1-pound bag will last quite a while, since these noodles expand greatly when cooked. Other ingredients that add volume and crunch that may be substituted are: shredded iceberg lettuce or crisp won ton noodles.

*CORNSTARCH is the traditional starch used for thickening sauces and coating foods in the Chinese kitchen. It is finer than flour and contains less protein, which accounts for its ability to add gloss and sheen to a sauce without muddying flavors. Purchase a 1-pound box and store in the pantry.

OILS, VINEGARS, AND SPIRITS

*PEANUT OIL is the favorite cooking oil of the Chinese kitchen. Because of its high smoking point and delicate flavor, it is perfect for all types of frying. **CORN OIL** may be used as a substitute. Although it also has a high burning point, its flavor is not as light.

*SESAME OIL, never used as a cooking oil in the Chinese kitchen, is used sparingly to add flavor and aroma to finished dishes and marinades. Made from roasted sesame seeds, it is dark brown with a distinctive nutty aroma. Do not substitute American sesame oil, which is made from raw seeds and has an entirely different flavor. Because there can be great variety in quality, purchase a small bottle of a higher-priced brand and store in a cool, dark place.

CHILI OIL is a fiery hot oil made from infusing vegetable oil with dried red chile peppers. It is traditionally placed on the table and added to dips for dim sum; it is also added in small quantities to Asian dressings and stuffings. Purchase a small bottle and store in a cool, dark place.

You can make your own by combining ½ cup corn or peanut oil and 2 tablespoons dried red chile flakes. Heat over moderate flame until the oil turns golden orange. Set aside to cool for 1 hour and strain into glass or plastic container.

*RICE VINEGAR is a mild, light vinegar used in dips, dressings, and as a flavoring for sweet and sour sauces. Marukan rice vinegar, sold in the supermarket in the oriental or gourmet section, is a good choice. Be sure to buy the "light and mild" type rather than the "gourmet seasoned" variety, which has added flavorings.

CHINESE BLACK VINEGAR or Chinkiang vinegar has a distinctive sweet, complex flavor slightly similar to Italian balsamic, although not as sweet. Because of its depth of flavor, it is frequently used in Szechuanese sauces. Since it is available only at Chinese markets, substitute apple cider vinegar or balsamic vinegar if necessary.

SHAO HSING, or Chinese rice wine, is the premier cooking wine of China. It is used in marinades, especially for fish and chicken, and sauces, usually in combination with soy sauce. It is available in Chinese markets, where it is surprisingly inexpensive. The only substitute is pale dry sherry, and an inexpensive supermarket brand is fine. Do not substitute sake, the Japanese rice wine, as the flavor is quite different.

BOTTLED SAUCES AND CONDIMENTS

A fundamental difference between European- and Asian-style cooking is found in sauce-making. Whereas the preparation of a hollandaise or beurre blanc may require several painstaking steps and an advanced degree in chemistry, Chinese sauce-making consists of combining prepared sauces and spices and then splashing them into the wok. While the resulting flavors may be complex, the cooking technique is simple. All of these special sauces are inexpensive and will store well, once opened, in the refrigerator.

*SOY SAUCE, the most important Chinese seasoning sauce, has become a staple of American- and European-style cooking in recent years. It is made of roasted soybean meal and wheat, naturally fermented, and then strained and bottled. If you are nervous about soy's sodium content, keep in mind that 1 teaspoon of soy contains 286 milligrams of sodium compared to the 2 grams in a teaspoon of salt. Soy not only adds a salty flavor to foods, it also enhances their natural flavors.

Chinese soy sauce is available in both a dark and a light or thin variety. For the recipes in this book, use either the Kikkoman brand sold in the supermarket or Chinese "superior" soy. For light soy sauce use Kikkoman (Thin) Light-Colored Soy Sauce, available in Chinese markets. This is not the same as low-sodium soy sauce.

Light soy sauce is saltier and is primarily used with light-colored foods like fish and vegetables, so they retain their light, bright color. If you are unable to find light soy, regular soy sauce is a fine substitute.

*HOISIN SAUCE, a thick, sweet sauce made of soy beans, wheat, garlic, vinegar, sugar, sesame seeds, and chiles is a popular ingredient in Chinese barbecued foods and stir-fried dishes. It also is placed on the table as a dipping sauce in restaurants serving dim sum and is the traditional condiment spread on pancakes with Peking duck and mu shu pork. It is worth purchasing several bottles of your favorite brand in a Chinese market, as it is used liberally for barbecuing and is easy to incorporate into daily cooking, especially with pork. Once opened, bottles can be stored in the refrigerator indefinitely.

*PLUM SAUCE is a sweet and sour chutneylike sauce similar to duck sauce. It is made of chunks of plum, ginger, and chiles mixed with vinegar and garlic. A popular Asian barbecue sauce ingredient, it also makes a delicious dip for fried dumplings and spring rolls. Once it is opened, store in the refrigerator.

*OYSTER SAUCE is a pungent brown sauce made of ground oysters, sugar, salt, and caramel. Use it sparingly in marinades and as a flavoring for sauces to go with noodles, chicken, and vegetable dishes. It is the traditional flavoring for steamed greens and broccoli. Store in the refrigerator once opened.

BEAN SAUCE OR GROUND BEAN SAUCE is a brown paste made of soy beans, salt, sugar, and flour. Its strong, salty flavor takes some getting used to. A trademark of northern and western Chinese cooking, bean sauce is often used in noodle and pork dishes. Use sparingly and balance with some sugar and chile peppers. Ground bean sauce is thought to be less desirable than plain bean sauce, though they may be used interchangeably. Purchase at a Chinese market and store indefinitely in the refrigerator. One bottle goes a long way.

CHINESE CHILI SAUCE OR CHILI GARLIC SAUCE is a bright red, fiery hot sauce containing red chile peppers, vinegar, and salt. It resembles a South American salsa in appearance and should be used with care in sauce and dips where a touch of fire is desired. On the West Coast Tuong Ot Toi Viet-nam brand, favored by restaurateurs and home cooks, has a picture of a rooster on the bottle. It is available in the ethnic section of some supermarkets and at Asian markets, and may be stored indefinitely in the refrigerator.

SPICES, SEASONINGS, AND HERBS

*GARLIC. Keep lots of garlic on hand for Chinese cooking, as it is a favorite seasoning of Asian chefs. As a rule purchase large, hard heads and store in a cool, dry place. For the recipes in this book, garlic cloves are always large and 1 tablespoon minced garlic equals 2 large cloves, minced. Garlic is native to Asia.

*GINGER. Second only to garlic as a seasoning agent is ginger. The combination of garlic and ginger, occasionally with scallions, provides the all-purpose Chinese seasoning. When finely minced and added to hot oil just before the main ingredients, they instantly lend a Chinese fragrance to whatever follows.

In Chinese cooking, ginger in the recipe always refers to the fresh root, rather than the dried, powdered form used for baking. Never substitute.

Fresh ginger can be purchased at the supermarket. Look for large, firm branches with smooth skin. Fresh, unpeeled ginger may be stored in a cool, dry place for up to 2 weeks. After that, it should be transferred to the vegetable bin of the refrigerator to prevent mold and wrinkling. If mold does occur, just trim and discard, and use the ginger that remains.

To mince ginger, cut in thin slices across the branch. Stack the slices and trim the skins. Then crush the fibers by whacking with the side of a cleaver and mince as you would garlic. For quantity it is easier to peel whole ginger with a sharp knife and then cut into ⅛-inch slices. Mince in a minichopper or food processor fitted with the steel blade. Minced ginger may be stored up to 3 weeks in the refrigerator in a sealed container with a small amount of rice vinegar or dry sherry to prevent drying.

*SCALLIONS OR GREEN ONIONS are frequently used as a seasoning, along with garlic and ginger. As a rule, the Chinese use the whole scallion, from the white bulb to the green stalks. The leafier green part is also thinly sliced and used as a garnish.

CILANTRO OR CHINESE PARSLEY is a distinctive, thin-leaved green herb similar in appearance to flat-leaf parsley but with a flavor all its own. A popular Mexican, Indian, and Asian ingredient, it is widely available in supermarkets. In the Chinese kitchen, cilantro is primarily used as a garnish, and although the tastes are quite different, Italian parsley or mint leaves may be used as a substitute. Since cilantro stems are so thin and digestible it is not necessary to remove them. Cilantro may be stored in the vegetable bin in the refrigerator up to 1 week, depending on freshness.

Before moving on to the more specialized spices, *salt, white pepper, and granulated sugar* should be mentioned as staples of Chinese cooking.

FIVE-SPICE POWDER is a ground spice mixture of star anise, cloves, cinnamon, fennel seed, and Szechuan peppercorns. It is rubbed over poultry or meats before roasting in southern Chinese cooking. It should be stored along with your other spices in a cool, dark place. Available in Chinese markets.

STAR ANISE is an 8-pointed, star-shaped pod with the distinctive strong flavor and aroma of licorice. It is added whole to braised dishes and stews. Purchase at Asian markets and store in sealed bottles in a cool, dark place.

CINNAMON BARK. A stick of cinnamon is often added to braised meat dishes, in combination with star anise, for a hint of sweet complexity. Although the Chinese variety, sometimes called cassia bark, is smaller and thinner than American stick cinnamon, the type sold in the super-market is perfectly acceptable.

DRIED RED CHILES, or chiles de arbol, used to add fire to Szechuan-style dishes such as kung pao chicken, can be purchased at most supermarkets. Always use sparingly as they are extremely spicy once heat releases their flavor. Store in a cool, dry place.

SZECHUAN PEPPERCORNS, also known as fagara, are reddish brown peppercorns that resemble an open seed with a tiny stem. They belong to an entirely different botanical family from black peppercorns and have a more delicate, elusive flavor and distinctive aroma. They are available in Chinese markets and should be stored along with your other spices.

To roast and grind Szechuan peppercorns: Place them in a small, dry skillet over medium heat and cook, shaking frequently, until they start to smoke. Remove from heat. Grind in a coffee grinder, spice mill, or minichopper until fine and then pass through a medium strainer to eliminate hard shells and stems. Roasted peppercorns may be stored in a sealed container in a cool, dry place up to 6 months.

DRIED PRESERVED INGREDIENTS

*SALTED OR FERMENTED BLACK BEANS are the key ingredient of southern Chinese black bean sauces. Since these small, black soybeans, fermented and preserved in salt, are extremely pungent, many cooks prefer to wash them before adding to dishes, although it is not necessary. They are always chopped and combined with minced garlic, ginger, and some wine before going into the wok. Black bean sauce is the common complement to fish and shellfish dishes. Available at Chinese markets; store in a sealed container in the refrigerator once opened.

PRESERVED RED GINGER SLICES IN SYRUP are bright red knobs of peeled ginger preserved in a sweet syrup, similar to canned fruit sauces. Both the ginger and the syrup add a refreshing, sweet, spicy flavor to Asian-style salads like Chinese chicken salad. Sold in bottles at Chinese markets, preserved red ginger should be stored in the refrigerator once opened.

PRESERVED OR CRYSTALLIZED GINGER is a traditional Chinese candy made of thin ginger slices processed with sugar and water. These pale orange, sugar-coated pieces have a refreshing, intensely spicy flavor. They are sold in the candy section of Chinese markets and may be stored indefinitely at room temperature.

*CHINESE DRIED BLACK MUSHROOMS are used with much greater frequency than fresh mushrooms in the Chinese kitchen. They add a strong woodsy flavor and spongy texture to many stir-fried dishes and soups. Chinese markets stock a large variety imported from all over Asia and they can range in price from reasonable to exorbitant, according to quality. A 2-ounce bag will last the average home cook quite a long time. They can be stored indefinitely in a cool, dark place. Japanese dried shiitake mushrooms, available at the supermarket, may be substituted.

Dried mushrooms should always be soaked in hot water to soften before cooking. Trim the tough stems and squeeze out excess water before slicing or chopping.

*TREE EAR OR CLOUD EAR MUSHROOMS are another form of dried fungi. These are much less flavorful than black mushrooms and more important for their slippery, chewy texture than their taste. They must be reconstituted in hot water like dried black mushrooms. Tree ears are sold at Chinese markets and may be stored indefinitely at room temperature.

CHINESE SWEET SAUSAGE OR LOP CHEUNG is sweet, hard sausage made of pork and pork fat. It is sold in packages of 10 links each in Chinese markets and may be stored, well wrapped, in the freezer once opened. They are delicious stir-fried, steamed, or grilled.

VEGETABLES

It is now possible to create authentic Chinese flavors with the vegetables available at most supermarkets. Aside from the more unusual vegetables, whose descriptions will follow, the following American staples are also indigenous to the Chinese kitchen: asparagus, broccoli, cucumbers, green beans or long beans, bean sprouts, spinach, watercress, leeks, and onions.

BOK CHOY has a long white stalk and leafy green top. Similar in appearance and texture to celery, it is a member of the cabbage family. Its delicious fresh, clean flavor is welcome in stir-fried dishes and soups. Bok choy is one of several stalk-type cabbages available at Chinese markets. It may be stored in the vegetable bin of the refrigerator up to 1 week.

NAPA CABBAGE, also known as celery cabbage, is a pale green, oval cabbage with thin, crinkly leaves. It is a popular addition to dim sum fillings, stir-fries, soups, and braised dishes. Its delicate flavor calls for minimum cooking and it is easily shredded by just rolling it into a cylinder and slicing thinly across the width. Store in the vegetable bin of the refrigerator where it will keep up to 2 weeks.

JAPANESE OR ORIENTAL EGGPLANT is the long, thin purple eggplant currently stocked by most supermarkets. Since it has fewer seeds, it holds less water and is therefore less bitter. It is not necessary to add salt or remove skins before cooking. Store in the refrigerator.

CHINESE SNOW PEAS are totally edible flat, green pea pods. Their sweet, delicate flavor and texture call for quick cooking. You need only trim the ends before cooking, since the string is not discernible. Sugar snap peas are a good substitute, but be sure to string them. Store in the vegetable bin of the refrigerator.

WATER CHESTNUTS are a brown-skinned water bulb native to China. They have an unmistakable sweet, refreshing flavor and crisp texture, quite different from the canned variety. At Chinese markets they are sometimes stored in water in the produce department, although the water is not necessary for home storage. Look for bulbs that are firm— soft spots indicate spoilage.

To prepare, wash off any mud under cold tap water. With a small paring knife, trim off the top and bottom and then peel the remaining brown skin with a circular motion. Rinse again to be sure all mud is removed. Store unpeeled water chestnuts, wrapped in plastic wrap, in the vegetable bin of the refrigerator where they will last a week or more depending on freshness. Jicama is a good substitute.

If you must use canned water chestnuts, rinse well and cook them briefly.

EQUIPMENT FOR THE CHINESE KITCHEN

If you plan on cooking Chinese food with any frequency, do not deprive yourself of the fun of owning a *wok*. Although it is possible to stir-fry in a large skillet, you can't bring the same reckless abandon to such a short-sided utensil. With a wok you can stir and toss the food and shake the pan vigorously without a worry—no food will land on the floor.

The best woks are also the least expensive. I prefer the heavy steel, round-bottomed, wooden-handled models sold in Chinese markets. If you have an electric range, you will need a flat-bottomed wok, sold by many department stores. Avoid electric woks, as they never get hot enough to truly stir-fry, but instead end up steaming the food.

Steel woks need to be seasoned first, much as you would a cast-iron pan. First scrub well with a scouring pad and soap and wipe dry. Place over medium-low heat, pour about 2 tablespoons of cooking oil on some paper towels, and coat the inside of the wok evenly. Heat for about 10 minutes, and then wipe again with paper towels. Repeat this procedure until the towels wipe clean. The seasoned pan will have a shiny black nonstick surface that improves with use. It is important when cleaning a seasoned wok not to scrub with soap or you will remove the finish. Just wipe clean with hot water and a nylon pad and then dry over a low flame.

If your wok does not come with them, purchase a *ring* and a *cover* for braising and steaming. Do not use the ring for stir-frying, but instead place the wok directly on the burner's grate for better heating. The ring, however, is very useful for holding the wok steady when braising or steaming.

As for stirring and tossing, I prefer *large, slotted spoons* for stir-frying, as I find Chinese triangular spatulas scratch the wok's surface. A *bamboo and metal net strainer*, though not necessary, is very convenient for lifting hot foods out of oil.

If you plan on using the wok for steaming, you may want to buy an inexpensive *circular steel rack* designed for that purpose. Plates of food fit above it and enough water rests below for perfect steaming. Also available at very little cost in Chinese markets are *heatproof ceramic bowls* for steaming.

Stacking bamboo steaming trays, seen in dim sum parlors, also fit well in the wok for steaming. However, make sure you line them with aluminum foil or cheesecloth before steaming delicate dumplings, or the wrappers may stick and tear. You may find they work better as kitchen ornaments than as utensils.

A disadvantage of using the wok for steaming is that a bit of the wok's seasoning layer will be removed by the boiling water. You can restore it easily enough by washing and then rubbing the inside of the wok with a tablespoon or so of oil and placing over low heat for about 15 minutes.

If you don't want to be bothered with reseasoning your wok, it is best to purchase a *large aluminum steamer* from a Chinese supply store for steaming whole fish and large platters of food. These are much less expensive than the stainless steel ones sold in department stores.

Considering the amount of time spent on preparation, a *good knife or cleaver* is essential for cooking Chinese food. While experienced Chinese chefs have 2 or 3 cleavers of differing weights, one good well-balanced, medium-sized cleaver with a blade measuring about 8 x 3 inches is really all you need. As with the wok, the cleaver is perfectly designed for its work in the kitchen. The flat of the blade can be used to crush garlic and ginger before mincing and as a scoop to transfer ingredients. And the blade is capable of cutting raw meats into the finest dice as well as chopping through recalcitrant poultry bones. As with all good knives, keep the blade sharpened and store where it cannot be damaged by other utensils.

An *electric rice cooker*, though not a necessity, is a great convenience if Asian cooking becomes a passion. Its main advantage, other than requiring no attention, is that it leaves the burners free for stir-frying. Consider buying one if you find yourself cooking Chinese food several times a week.

SOUPS

IN CHINA, SOUP IS SIPPED THROUGHOUT THE MEAL, MUCH LIKE TEA. AT HOME AND IN RUSTIC-STYLE RESTAURANTS, A SIMPLE BROTH IS USUALLY SERVED, WHILE THE REPERTOIRE OF SOUPS AVAILABLE AT FINE RESTAURANTS NUMBERS IN THE HUNDREDS. BROTH IS THE VEHICLE FOR TWO OF THE MOST PRIZED TEXTURE INGREDIENTS—SHARK'S FIN AND BIRD'S NEST. HERE IS A SMALL SAMPLE OF SIMPLE BROTHS, ALL EASILY ACCESSIBLE TO THE HOME COOK.

CHINESE CHICKEN STOCK

Chinese chicken broth has fewer distractions than European-style broths—just the pure, rich taste of chicken with an undercurrent of ginger. Although it is fine to use canned broth for daily stir-frying, if you are going to take the time to make a Chinese soup, it is worth the effort to make this broth first. The resulting soup will have a much more authentic flavor.

Chicken feet, a time-honored enricher of ethnic chicken soups, can be purchased at most Chinese markets. ✖ *Makes 10 cups*

3½ pounds assorted chicken parts
  including backs, wings, and feet
Cold water to cover
3 scallions, white and green, cut
  in 1-inch lengths

1 inch chunk unpeeled fresh
  ginger, cut in 6 slices
1 tablespoon salt

1] Wash the chicken parts and place in a large stockpot. Bring to the stove and pour in enough cold water to cover. Add the scallions, ginger, and salt and bring to a boil. When the water is boiling briskly, skim and discard the foam that rises to the surface. Reduce the heat to a simmer and cook, uncovered, 2½ hours. Check the pot and skim foam every ½ hour. Set aside to cool.

2] Strain the stock and store in sealed containers in the refrigerator for up to 5 days or in the freezer for 6 months. Before using, remove and discard the layer of fat from the top.

CRAB AND
SNOW PEA SOUP

This easy, elegant soup would make an excellent starter for an American meal of grilled chops and steamed vegetables. ✗ *Serves 4*

1 generous cup cooked crab meat
  (about ¾ pound with shell), or
  ½ pound meat only
4 cups Chinese Chicken Stock (see
  page 23)
4 ounces snow peas, trimmed and
  julienned

1 egg, beaten
1 tablespoon cornstarch mixed
  with 1 tablespoon water
1 teaspoon sesame oil
2 teaspoons dry sherry
½ teaspoon salt
½ teaspoon white pepper

1] Prepare the crab by removing the shells and tearing the meat into large chunks. Carefully pick over the meat for bits of shell. Have all of the ingredients ready near the stove.

2] Bring the chicken stock to a boil in a stockpot or large saucepan. Add the snow peas and cook over medium-high heat for 2 minutes.

3] Reduce the heat to medium-low. Stir a teaspoon or two of hot broth into the beaten egg and then add to the broth in a slow, steady stream. As you are adding the egg, stir the broth briskly to disperse evenly into egg drop threads. Then add the cornstarch mixture and cook an additional minute. Turn off the heat.

4] Stir in the crab meat and remaining ingredients. Adjust seasonings to taste and serve hot.

VARIATION. Another classic combination is corn and crab meat. Add kernels from 2 ears of corn along with the snow peas.

BARBECUED DUCK AND LEEK SOUP

This rustic one-dish meal captures the soulful spirit of Chinese home cooking. If barbecued duck is not available, substitute strips of barbecued chicken, pork, or beef. ✖ *Serves 4*

4 ounces bean threads or rice sticks
5 dried Chinese black mushrooms
6 cups Chinese Chicken Stock (see page 23)
2 leeks, white part, cut in half lengthwise and washed

½ Chinese barbecued duck
2 cups bean sprouts
Salt and white pepper

1] Fill a large mixing bowl with hot tap water and soak the dried bean threads or rice sticks for 15 minutes. Drain, rinse with cold water, and drain again. Reserve.

2] Soak the mushrooms in hot water for 15 minutes. Then remove the stems and thinly slice the caps.

3] Meanwhile bring the stock to a boil in a stockpot or large saucepan.

4] Cut the white part of the leeks in half again across the width. Thinly slice lengthwise into julienne.

5] Remove the duck meat by running a sharp knife between meat and bone. Cut into thin strips, leaving the skin on.

6] When the broth is boiling, add the bean threads, leeks, and mushrooms. Reduce to a simmer and cook, uncovered, 10 minutes. Add the shredded duck and bean sprouts and simmer an additional 3 minutes, just to heat through. Taste and adjust seasonings with salt and pepper. Serve hot, with spoons and chopsticks or forks for the noodles.

Chinese Cooking for Beginners

HOT AND SOUR SOUP

Once all the ingredients are cut and measured, this classic soup takes minutes to prepare. Adjust the seasoning mixture to taste after adding it to the broth. ✖ *Serves 4*

4 cups Chinese Chicken Stock (see page 23)
1 skinless boneless chicken breast (½ pound), sliced paper-thin along the grain
3 large tree ear mushrooms, soaked in hot water 15 minutes and thinly sliced
2 ounces bamboo shoots, julienned (½ cup)
5 ounces firm tofu, thinly sliced and julienned (1 cup)

SEASONINGS_____
2 tablespoons Chinese black vinegar or distilled white vinegar
1 tablespoon soy sauce
½ teaspoon black pepper
1 teaspoon chili oil
_____
2 tablespoons cornstarch mixed with 2 tablespoons water
1 egg beaten with 1 teaspoon sesame oil

1] Bring the chicken stock to a boil in a large saucepan or stockpot. Have all of the sliced ingredients ready on a nearby platter and mix the seasoning ingredients together in a bowl.

2] Add the shredded chicken, tree ears, bamboo shoots, and tofu to the boiling stock. Reduce the heat and simmer about 3 minutes.

3] Stir in the seasonings. Bring back to a boil and then pour in the cornstarch mixture in a slow, steady stream. Stir for about a minute while the soup thickens.

4] Turn off the heat. Pour in the beaten egg, stirring constantly to break into egg drop shreds. Serve hot.

VARIATIONS. About 1½ cups shredded pork can be substituted for chicken. If you prefer more vegetables, slivered carrots or shredded spinach or cabbage can be added at the same time as the chicken.

WON TON SOUP

───────■───────

In China, won ton soup is considered a small meal or snack rather than a course to be taken before dinner. Suggestions are included for making the broth as substantial or colorful as you wish, though it is equally lovely with only the dumplings, or clouds, floating in clear broth. In Chinese, *won ton* means "swallowing clouds." ✖ *Serves 4*

FILLING
6 ounces ground pork
3 scallions, white and green, finely chopped
3 water chestnuts, washed, peeled, and finely chopped
1 teaspoon minced fresh ginger
1 teaspoon light soy sauce
¼ teaspoon salt
¼ teaspoon sugar
¼ teaspoon white pepper
½ teaspoon sesame oil

About 20 won ton or dumpling skins
4 cups Chinese Chicken Stock (see page 23)
¼ pound medium shrimp, shelled and deveined (optional)
2 scallions, white and green, thinly sliced, for garnish
Salt and white pepper

Optional garnishes: barbecued pork or chicken, diced honey cured ham, bamboo shoots

1] Place the ground pork in a medium mixing bowl. Add the chopped scallions and water chestnuts along with the remaining filling ingredients and combine well. The best tools for combining are your hands.

2] Have a small bowl of cold water nearby for sealing the dough. Arrange a batch of won ton skins on the counter. Spoon about a teaspoon of filling in the center of each. With a fingertip dipped in water, moisten 2 edges that form a right angle. Fold over, creating a triangle, and press the edges together to seal. Then moisten the 2 opposite points of dough and press together to form a little cap. Reserve the dumplings on a cornstarch-dusted plate.

3] Meanwhile fill a large pasta pot with water for cooking the dumplings. In another pot bring the chicken stock to a simmer.

4] To cook shrimp, salt the large pot of boiling water and toss in the shrimp. Cook until pink, about 1 minute, and transfer with a slotted spoon or bamboo strainer to the pot of simmering stock. Also add the scallions and any other garnishes to the chicken stock at this time. Taste and adjust with salt and pepper.

5] Add the won tons to the pot of boiling water, one at a time, with your hand close to the water's surface to avoid splashing. Gently stir to avoid sticking. Cook until the won tons rise to the surface, about a minute. Then, with a strainer or slotted spoon, transfer them to the soup pot. Cook at low heat for 2 additional minutes and serve. Won ton soup tastes best eaten immediately, before the skins get soggy and tear as they absorb more broth.

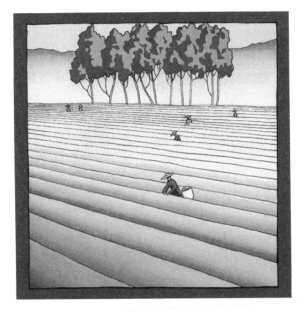

MINIATURE LION'S HEAD SOUP

Traditional lion's heads are huge meatballs braised on a bed of cabbage. This quick adaptation, inspired by Mary Sue Milliken and Susan Feniger of City Restaurant in Los Angeles, makes a substantial one-dish meal. ✕ *Serves 6*

3 tree ear mushrooms
2 ounces bean thread noodles

MEATBALLS_____
½ pound ground pork
1 teaspoon minced garlic
1 teaspoon minced fresh ginger
1 tablespoon soy sauce
1 tablespoon minced water
  chestnut or jicama

6 cups Chinese Chicken Stock (see
  page 23)
3 cups shredded Napa cabbage
¼ teaspoon white pepper
1 teaspoon sesame oil
1 teaspoon soy sauce
4 scallions, white and green,
  thinly sliced, for garnish

1] Soak the tree ears and the bean threads in individual bowls of hot tap water until reconstituted, about 15 minutes. Drain and thinly slice the mushrooms. Drain and chop the noodles into 4-inch lengths.

2] Combine all of the meatball ingredients in a bowl. Form small balls by rolling about a teaspoon of the mixture between your palms. Reserve on a platter.

3] Bring the chicken stock to a boil in a large saucepan or stockpot. Add the meatballs, tree ears, bean threads, and Napa cabbage. Reduce to a simmer and cook, uncovered, about 10 minutes. Stir in the white pepper, sesame oil, and soy. Taste and adjust seasonings. Ladle into bowls and sprinkle with scallions.

DIM SUM, APPETIZERS, AND SALADS

These dishes represent a thoroughly American take on Chinese cooking, since appetizers do not exist in the traditional Chinese meal. In the typical home-style meal, entrée, appetizer, soup, and vegetables are served at the same time, with each diner helping himself in whatever order he or she may choose.

For the American cook, however, the appetizer course is a comfortable place to begin experimenting with Chinese cooking. Many of these dishes do not require last-minute stir-frying and so can be prepared at least partially in advance. The roasted and barbecued meats employ familiar techniques, as do the salads. And while it may take some practice to master dim sum, they deliver a big payoff since everybody loves eating them.

Folding dumplings is one of those techniques, like kneading bread, where experience is the best teacher. If you have the opportunity to take a class or observe dumplings being folded in an open kitchen, it will greatly help you to produce neatly folded dumplings first time out. Once you get the knack, of course, the trick is to enlist the help of friends and family as the Chinese do, to make the job more fun. Serve small plates of soy sauce, rice vinegar, chili oil, mustard, and plum sauce for dipping dumplings at the table.

DIM SUM AND APPETIZERS

CLASSIC OPEN-FACED DUMPLINGS

With its open face and loose pleats, shau mai, the classic Cantonese dumpling, is the easiest to fold. Serve with small dishes of soy sauce, chili oil, and rice vinegar for dipping. If round won ton skins are unavailable, just stack the square ones and trim the corners with a sharp knife. ✖ *Makes 24 dumplings*

½ pound medium shrimp, shelled and deveined
1 egg white
4 dried Chinese black mushrooms, soaked in hot water 15 minutes
¼ pound ground pork
6 water chestnuts, peeled and minced
4 scallions, white and green, minced
1 teaspoon minced fresh ginger

1 tablespoon dry sherry
2 teaspoons light soy sauce
½ teaspoon salt
¼ teaspoon white pepper
¼ teaspoon sugar
1 teaspoon sesame oil
½ teaspoon chili oil
24 round won ton or Japanese gyoza skins, about 9 ounces
Peanut oil for brushing

1] Place the cleaned shrimp on a chopping board. Pour on the egg white and roughly chop, incorporating the egg as you go. Do not chop too fine—large chunks will add a nice texture to the finished dumplings. Transfer to a medium bowl.

2] Drain and mince the reconstituted mushrooms, discarding tough stems. Add the mushrooms and all the remaining ingredients, except the wrappers and peanut oil, to the shrimp in the bowl. Combine well. This stuffing can be covered with plastic wrap and reserved in the refrigerator for several hours.

3] To fill the dumplings, have a small bowl of cold water nearby and dust a platter with cornstarch. Working in batches, arrange the round won ton skins on a counter. With a finger dipped in water, moisten the outside edge. Place about a tablespoon of filling in the center of each.

Then gather the top edges in one hand and lift, squeezing the top in the curve between thumb and index finger. By so doing pleats should form along the top edge. With your other hand, press down the filling at the top and tamp the bottom with a thumb to flatten. Stuffed dumplings may be reserved on the platter in the refrigerator for up to 2 hours.

4] To steam, if using a bamboo tray, cover it with aluminum foil so air circulates through small openings on either side. Lightly coat the foil (or whatever surface you are using) with peanut oil to avoid sticking and arrange dumplings on top.

5] Fill a wok or large saucepan with water to about an inch beneath the steaming tray. Bring to a rapid boil. Place the steaming tray on top, cover, and reduce the heat to medium. Cook until the pork loses its pinkness, about 10 minutes. Tip dumplings onto a serving platter and serve with assorted dips.

SAVORY CHICKEN POT STICKERS

Ask the butcher to grind chicken thighs for you, since dark meat is what makes these little dumplings so moist and hearty. A nonstick pan is essential for making perfect pot stickers. ✖ *Makes 28 to 32 dumplings*

10 ounces ground chicken,
   preferably thigh meat
4 scallions, white and green,
   minced
1 carrot, peeled and minced
1½ teaspoons minced fresh ginger
½ teaspoon minced garlic
1 tablespoon light soy sauce
1 teaspoon sesame oil
½ teaspoon salt

½ teaspoon white pepper
¼ to ½ teaspoon Chinese chili
   sauce, to taste
¼ teaspoon sugar
32 round won ton or Japanese
   gyoza skins
¼ cup peanut oil
½ cup chicken stock or water
Rice vinegar, soy sauce, and chili
   oil for dipping

1] In a mixing bowl, combine all of the ingredients except the won tons, peanut oil, chicken stock, and dipping liquids. Mix well.

2] To fill the dumplings, have a small bowl of cold water nearby. Arrange a few dumpling wrappers at a time on a clean counter. Place about 2 teaspoons of filling in the center of each and shape to form a long, thin cylinder of filling.

With the tip of your index finger, moisten the top inside edge of the wrapper. Gather and pinch together one corner and lift the dumpling in order to work with it in the palm of your hand. On the side closest to you, make about 3 pleats, pinching and pressing wrapper to the opposite edge to enclose the filling. (As long as the filling is enclosed, don't worry too much about appearances. Just wipe off any filling that may ooze out between the folds and use less filling until you get the knack.) When the dumpling is sealed, gently curl it in a crescent shape as you place it on a platter.

3] To cook, heat the oil in a 12-inch nonstick skillet over medium-high heat. Add the dumplings one at a time, arranging them tightly in rows. Cook until the bottoms turn golden brown, about 7 minutes. (Pick one up occasionally to check.)

4] Pour in the stock or water, cover, and cook at medium heat until the skins become translucent, about 3 minutes. Remove the cover and continue cooking until the liquid in the pan evaporates, about 6 minutes. As pot stickers are finishing, toss or stir to loosen the bottoms. The bottoms should be dark brown when done. Tip onto a serving platter and serve hot with rice vinegar, soy sauce, and chili oil for dipping.

BOILED GINGER
SCALLOP DUMPLINGS

‎■

These boiled dumplings have a clean, bracing flavor from the ginger and lemon. ✕ *Makes 28 to 30 dumplings*

½ pound bay or sea scallops
1 small egg white
3 scallions, white and green,
   minced
1 teaspoon dry sherry
1 teaspoon sesame oil
½ teaspoon grated lemon zest
½ teaspoon minced fresh ginger

1 teaspoon cornstarch
About 30 round or square won ton
   or gyoza wrappers

DRESSING
2 tablespoons light soy sauce
2 tablespoons rice vinegar
1 scallion, thinly sliced

1] Combine the scallops with the egg white on a cutting board and chop finely. Dumplings taste better with larger bits of meat, so don't be too finicky. Place in a mixing bowl with the remaining ingredients except the wrappers and dressing. Combine well. The filling can be reserved in the refrigerator, covered, for up to 2 hours.

2] To fill dumplings, have a small bowl of water ready nearby and a baking tray dusted with cornstarch. Center a generous teaspoonful of filling on each skin. (It is easiest to work in batches.) With a finger dipped in water, moisten the outside edge of half of the wrapper. Fold over, pressing the dry dough to the wet to seal and enclose the filling. Then, lifting in your hands, moisten one tip and press the 2 points together to form a small cap. Reserve on cornstarch-dusted tray in the refrigerator until cooking time. These can be stuffed several hours in advance.

3] Combine the dressing in a small bowl. To cook the dumplings, bring a large saucepan or stockpot of water to a boil. Salt the water as you would for pasta, and drop in the dumplings. Stir the dumplings once to avoid sticking and cook until they all rise to the top and bubble there for about 10 seconds.

4] Drain in a colander, shaking vigorously to remove excess water. Do not be concerned with dumplings that may have lost some filling. Tip out onto a deep platter or bowl, pour on the dressing, and gently toss. Serve immediately.

FRIED LAMB WON TONS

These hearty fried dumplings make wonderful finger foods to serve with cocktails or at an informal buffet. You can fold them in the morning and fry before serving. Cooking time is about 5 minutes.

✖ *Makes about 36 dumplings*

5 ounces (3 cups) spinach leaves, washed
½ pound ground lamb
1 large carrot, peeled and diced
1½ tablespoons minced chives
1 tablespoon minced fresh ginger
1 tablespoon minced garlic
1 tablespoon soy sauce
1 tablespoon dry sherry

¼ teaspoon Chinese chili sauce
½ teaspoon salt
¼ teaspoon white pepper
1 egg, beaten
36 square won ton skins (about 9 ounces)
1½ cups vegetable or peanut oil
Plum sauce and rice vinegar for dipping

1] Bring 1 or 2 inches of salted water to a boil in a medium saucepan. Stir in the spinach and cook until wilted, less than a minute. Drain in a colander and rinse with cold water. Press out excess moisture with your hands. Roughly chop.

2] Combine the spinach with the lamb and the remaining ingredients except the won tons, frying oil, and dipping liquids.

3] To fill won tons, follow the instructions on page 28 for won ton soup. Like all dumplings, they may be reserved on an uncovered platter dusted with cornstarch for up to 8 hours in the refrigerator.

4] Heat the oil to 350 F in a 10-inch skillet. Line counters with paper towels for draining. Test the oil by dropping in a sliver of won ton skin. When the oil is hot enough, the won ton will remain at the surface, turning brown and crisp. If it blackens immediately, lower the heat and let the oil cool a bit. Cook in batches until golden brown on one side. Then turn with tongs and brown the other side, about 1 minute altogether. Transfer to paper towels to drain.

5] Serve hot with Chinese plum sauce and rice vinegar for dipping.

Shrimp and Vegetable Spring Rolls

The key to foolproof spring rolls is to stir-fry the stuffing a day in advance and then chill before rolling. Spring roll skins are available in the freezer section of Asian markets. Although they look delicate, they are actually quite sturdy and need to be pulled apart forcefully after defrosting to separate the skins. If you can't find spring roll skins, substitute egg roll skins from the supermarket. These are also delicious without the shrimp, for vegetarian rolls. *Makes 12 large rolls*

½ pound cooked small shrimp
2 cups bean sprouts
1 cup shredded Napa cabbage
2 cups slivered carrots
2 stalks broccoli, tops only, cut into small florets
4 dried Chinese black mushrooms, soaked in hot water 15 minutes, drained, and thinly sliced
2 scallions, white and green, cut in 2-inch lengths and sliced lengthwise

SAUCE

1 tablespoon light soy sauce
1 tablespoon dry sherry
2 teaspoons oyster sauce
2 teaspoons sesame oil

---

2 tablespoons peanut oil
2 teaspoons minced garlic
2 teaspoons minced fresh ginger
1 teaspoon coarse salt
12 spring roll or egg roll skins, defrosted in the refrigerator
1 egg, beaten
3 cups peanut oil, for deep-frying
Plum sauce and soy sauce for dipping

1] Combine the shrimp with all of the prepared vegetables in a large mixing bowl. Combine the sauce ingredients in a small bowl.

2] Heat the 2 tablespoons of peanut oil in a wok or very large (14-inch) skillet over high heat. Sauté the garlic and ginger for a few seconds and then add shrimp and vegetable mixture. Stir-fry, with the coarse salt, over high heat about 2 minutes.

3] Pour in the sauce ingredients, toss well, and cook about 30 seconds more. Remove from heat. Transfer to a bowl and set aside to cool. Cover and refrigerate a minimum of 6 hours or up to a day in advance.

4] To stuff the spring rolls, have ready the beaten egg, a brush, and a tray or platter dusted with cornstarch. Drain the chilled stuffing mixture of excess moisture.

One at a time, place the wrappers on a clean counter, laid out with a point facing you, like diamond shapes. Arrange a generous ¼ cup of stuffing lengthwise along the lower half of the diamond, leaving about 1 inch of wrapper on either side uncovered. Fold up the lower corner to cover the filling and fold again to enclose. Tamp down the sides to make a packet of the filling in the center. Coat excess wrapper on both sides of the filling with egg and fold toward the center to seal.

Brush the unrolled edges of wrapper with egg, then roll and press to fully enclose. Reserve on cornstarch-dusted platter at room temperature, covered with a dry towel, up to 1 hour. Do not refrigerate or the skins will crack.

5] To cook, heat the 3 cups of oil to 325 F in a 10-inch skillet. Drop in a sliver of spring roll skin to test. Fry the rolls in batches of about 4 until golden brown all over, about 1 minute per side for spring rolls and 2½ minutes per side for egg rolls. Use tongs for turning. Drain on paper towels and serve hot with Chinese plum sauce for dipping.

Chinese Cooking for Beginners

HOT SHRIMP WITH SOY SCALLION DIP

Go to the trouble of purchasing the freshest shrimp for this simple preparation and you won't be disappointed. ✖ *Serves 6*

1 pound large or medium shrimp, in the shell
3 tablespoons soy sauce
1 teaspoon rice wine vinegar

2 scallions, white and green, thinly sliced
1 tablespoon peanut oil
¼ teaspoon chili oil
1 teaspoon salt

1] Set a large pot of water up to boil. Meanwhile, wash the shrimp in a large strainer under cold running water. Do not remove the shells.

2] To prepare the dip, combine the soy sauce, rice wine vinegar, and scallions in a small ceramic serving bowl. Place the peanut and chili oils in a small pan and cook over medium heat about 3 minutes. Pour into the scallion mixture.

3] When the water comes to a rapid boil, add the salt and the shrimp. Reduce heat to medium and cook 3 minutes. To test for doneness, remove a shrimp, rinse it under cold water, peel, and taste. Transfer cooked shrimp with a bamboo strainer or slotted spoon to a serving bowl. Do not rinse.

4] Bring the hot shrimp and dip to the table, along with a bowl for the shells and plenty of napkins.

BITE-SIZED GARLIC SPARE RIBS

These miniature ribs are easier to serve at picnics or buffets than the larger ones—they only require one hand. In China, ribs are traditionally served this size. ✖ *Serves 6*

MARINADE_____
½ cup hoisin sauce
¼ cup rice vinegar
2 tablespoons plum sauce
2 tablespoons soy sauce
1 tablespoon sesame oil
2 teaspoons chili oil
1½ tablespoons honey

¼ cup minced garlic (about 8 cloves)
6 scallions, white and green, sliced

_____

3¾ pounds pork spareribs, cut across the bones into 1½-inch-wide strips

1] Combine all of the marinade ingredients in a large bowl or ceramic pan. Add the ribs and rub them all over with the marinade. Cover with plastic wrap and refrigerate 8 to 24 hours.

2] Preheat oven to 350 F. Line a large roasting pan with aluminum foil for easy cleaning. Coat the rack with peanut oil. Wipe off the marinade and reserve it. Arrange the ribs on the rack.

3] Bake ½ hour and then turn and brush with the marinade. Bake ½ hour more and set aside to cool 5 minutes. With a cleaver or sharp knife, chop each strip apart between the bones for bite-sized serving pieces. Serve hot or at room temperature.

SPICY BARBECUED CHICKEN WINGS

Chicken wings and feet are prized ingredients in the Chinese kitchen. ✗ *Serves* 8

4 pounds chicken wings

MARINADE_____
1 cup hoisin sauce
⅓ cup plum sauce
¼ cup soy sauce
¼ cup dry sherry
¼ cup rice vinegar

½ cup orange juice
2 tablespoons honey
4 garlic cloves, peeled and
   chopped
1 inch length peeled ginger, grated
1 teaspoon cracked black pepper

1] Wash the chicken and pat dry. Combine all the marinade ingredients in a large bowl. Add the chicken wings and toss to coat evenly with marinade. Cover with plastic wrap and refrigerate at least 8 hours, or as long as a day. Remove from refrigerator ½ hour before cooking.

2] Preheat oven to 350 F. Line a roasting pan with aluminum foil for easier cleanup and coat a rack with peanut oil. Lift the chicken out of the marinade, wiping off excess, and arrange on the rack. Reserve the marinade.

3] Roast, uncovered, ½ hour on each side. Baste with the marinade at 15-minute intervals. After removing from oven, turn on the broiler.

4] When the broiler is hot, place the wings under broiler for 2 minutes on each side, just to crisp. Serve hot or at room temperature.

ASIAN SEAFOOD SALAD

━━━━━━━━━■━━━━━━━━━

This beautiful salad makes an impressive main course for a special lunch or light supper. You can prepare the seafood and the salad in advance. Chill separately and then toss with the dressing just before serving. ✗ *Serves 4*

¾ pound medium shrimp, bay scallops, or cooked crab meat, or any combination
3 tablespoons lemon juice
10 ounces (6 cups) spinach, washed and dried
4 ounces (2 cups) watercress, washed and dried
1 red bell pepper, cored and seeded

5 ounces jicama, peeled
¼ cup slivered red sweet ginger

DRESSING_____
3 tablespoons safflower oil
3 tablespoons rice wine vinegar
1 tablespoon syrup from red sweet ginger
2 teaspoons chili oil
½ teaspoon salt

1] If using fresh shrimp, shell and devein. Bring a large pot of water to a boil with some salt and cook the shrimp or scallops just until they turn white, about 1 minute. Drain and rinse well with cold water to stop the cooking. Sprinkle with lemon juice and chill.

2] Remove any tough stems from the spinach and watercress and chop into large pieces. Slice the red pepper and jicama into thin strips, or julienne.

3] If serving immediately, combine the greens with the red pepper, jicama, and red ginger strips. Toss well. Add the chilled seafood and toss again.

4] Whisk the dressing ingredients together in a small bowl. Pour over the salad, toss well, and serve.

CHINESE CHICKEN SALAD

This light, crunchy, sweet and sour chicken salad has become a staple of American restaurant dining—like the Caesar, Waldorf, and cobb salads of previous generations.

✘ *Serves 4 as an appetizer or 2 as an entrée*

1 medium head iceberg lettuce
2 cups slivered carrots
1 cup bean sprouts
One 2½-pound barbecued or
    roasted chicken
1 cup slivered almonds
1¼ cups corn or peanut oil
15 won ton skins

DRESSING
2 scallions, white and green, in
    2-inch pieces

1 garlic clove, peeled
3 inches sweet red ginger
2 tablespoons sesame oil
2 tablespoons peanut oil
3 tablespoons red wine vinegar
1 tablespoon light soy sauce
4 teaspoons syrup from red ginger
¼ teaspoon chili oil
¼ teaspoon salt

1] Preheat the oven to 325 F.

2] Cut the lettuce in quarters and remove the core. Thinly slice. Combine the lettuce, carrots, and bean sprouts in a salad bowl. Cut the chicken in half. Remove the skin and bones and cut the chicken into bite-sized pieces. Toss with the salad. Reserve in the refrigerator.

3] Spread the almonds on a baking sheet and toast in the warm oven, shaking occasionally, until golden, about 10 minutes. Reserve.

4] Heat the corn or peanut oil in a 10-inch skillet over high heat. Slice the won tons into ½-inch-wide strips. Test the oil by dropping in a won ton strip. If it turns golden within seconds the oil is ready.

5] Fry the won tons in batches, stirring to separate the pieces and turn, until golden all over, 30 seconds. Drain on paper towels. These burn easily so watch closely. Reserve until serving time.

6] To make the dressing, fit a food processor with the metal blade. Turn on the motor and add the scallions, garlic, and red ginger through the feed tube. Process until finely minced. Add the remaining ingredients and process until a smooth dressing or emulsion is formed. Taste and

7] Assemble the salad just before serving. Pour the dressing over the combined salad ingredients and toss well. Add the toasted nuts and won ton slivers and gently toss just to combine.

BARBECUED DUCK
SALAD

==========■==========

If barbecued duck is unavailable, substitute half a barbecued chicken in this rich salad. ✖ *Serves 4*

½ Chinese barbecued duck
1 large mango, peeled, or
   2 peaches
1 medium head romaine lettuce,
   washed and dried
1 pickling cucumber, peeled
3 scallions, white and green, cut
   in 1-inch lengths
1 cup vegetable oil
1 ounce rice sticks

DRESSING_____
1 garlic clove, peeled and minced
3 tablespoons safflower oil
3 tablespoons rice wine vinegar
1 teaspoon sesame oil
2 teaspoons honey
½ teaspoon salt
¼ teaspoon white pepper

1] Remove the duck meat from the bone, leaving the skin on. Cut into slivers across the grain.

2] If using mango, a tricky fruit to slice, first peel the skin with a knife. Then, with a sharp knife, make lengthwise cuts through the fruit to the pit. Remove the meat by running the blade between the pit and fruit. If using peaches, cut in half, remove the pits and thinly slice.

3] Cut the lettuce into thin strips by gathering a few leaves at a time and rolling them into a cylinder, lengthwise. Cut across the roll at ¼-inch intervals. Fluff with your fingers to separate.

4] Cut the cucumber in half lengthwise and remove the seeds. Thinly slice across the width. Combine the lettuce, cucumbers, and scallions in a large salad bowl and chill.

5] Heat the oil in a large skillet over high heat. Break the rice sticks into 5 or 6 batches. Test the oil by dropping in a rice stick. If it puffs immediately the oil is ready. Cook in batches until puffy, a few seconds per side. Drain on paper towels and then break into 1-inch lengths.

6] When ready to serve, whisk the dressing ingredients together in a small bowl. Toss with the salad ingredients to coat well. Add the slivered duck, fruit, and rice sticks. Gently toss and serve.

POULTRY, MEAT, AND FISH

In assembling such a small selection from the vast repertoire of Chinese entrées, I tried to include something for everyone, while remaining true to the Chinese preference for small quantities of pork, poultry, and fish in the diet. There are nostalgic restaurant favorites such as Sweet and Sour Pork, popular dishes such as Mu Shu Pork and Kung Pau Chicken, and newer, lighter improvisations such as Chicken with Corn and Wild Mushrooms and Shrimp and Leeks. Most take no longer than 10 minutes to cook once the prep work is done, and make a satisfying supper when served with plain white rice.

If you have not yet tried cooking fish Chinese-style, you are in for a revelation. Exotic-sounding dishes such as Monkfish with Sizzling Chili Oil or Steamed Snapper with Ginger and Scallions are exceptionally quick and easy to prepare and make delightful meals when served with a simple salad or stir-fried greens and rice.

SOY-BRAISED CHICKEN

Soy-braising results in an exceptionally tender, moist bird with a glossy burnished skin. This style, known as "red cooking," is typical of Fukien, the southern coastal city known for the best soy sauce. Chinese chefs save the leftover sauce mixture, called a master sauce, and reuse it in other soy-braised foods. ✕ *Serves 4*

One 3-pound chicken, preferably a
   roaster
Salt
½ cup soy sauce
½ cup dry sherry
2 tablespoons hoisin sauce
1 tablespoon sugar

2 star anise
1 cup water
2 tablespoons peanut oil
1 tablespoon minced garlic
1 tablespoon minced fresh ginger
Sesame oil for brushing
Fresh cilantro sprigs for garnish

1] Wash the chicken and pat dry. Sprinkle inside and out with salt. In a medium mixing bowl, mix together the soy sauce, sherry, hoisin sauce, sugar, star anise, and water.

2] Heat the peanut oil in a wok over high heat. Brown the chicken on all sides and transfer to a platter.

3] Stir-fry the garlic and ginger just until their fragrance is released, less than a minute. Pour in the soy mixture and bring to a boil. Add the chicken, breast side down, and reduce to a simmer. Cover and cook for 20 minutes. Turn chicken on its back and cook, covered, another 20 minutes. Turn off the heat and let sit with the cover on 15 minutes. Transfer the chicken to a cutting board and brush all over with sesame oil.

4] To serve Chinese style, first remove the legs and wings and cut them again at the joints for smaller pieces. Then make a cut on either side of the breastbone and chop through the back to split in half. Remove the breast meat on each side in one piece and chop each across the grain into bite-sized pieces. Arrange the pieces on a platter and garnish with cilantro sprigs. Serve hot or at room temperature.

Minced Chicken Breast in Lettuce Cups

These sweet and crunchy lettuce cups are a great weeknight family meal. Although the recipe may look long, it is easy to prepare. Lettuce cups also make an elegant appetizer, if you roll them before serving.

Serves 4

½ pound boneless, skinless chicken breasts

Marinade

1 teaspoon light soy sauce
1 teaspoon dry sherry
¼ teaspoon salt
⅛ teaspoon white pepper

2 dried Chinese black mushrooms
1 carrot, peeled and diced
¼ cup diced water chestnuts or jicama
2 scallions, white and green, thinly sliced

Sauce

2 tablespoons oyster sauce
1 tablespoon light soy sauce
½ tablespoon dry sherry
¼ teaspoon sugar
½ teaspoon sesame oil

1 large garlic clove, peeled and minced
1 large head iceberg lettuce, or 8 leaves, washed
2 cups plus 1 tablespoon peanut oil
1 ounce rice sticks

1] Cut the chicken into paper-thin strips lengthwise and then roughly chop. Place in a mixing bowl and combine with the marinade ingredients. Let sit at room temperature 20 minutes.

2] Meanwhile soak the mushrooms in hot tap water for 15 minutes. When the mushrooms are soft, drain, trim and discard the stems, and coarsely chop caps. Place all the chopped vegetables on a platter near the stove.

3] Mix the sauce ingredients in a small bowl and place near the stove, along with the garlic for stir-frying.

4] Prepare the lettuce cups for serving by halving the lettuce close to the core. Remove and discard any wilted outer leaves. Carefully peel the large, outer leaves and arrange 2 on each of 4 serving plates.

5] Heat 2 cups of the oil in a wok or large skillet over high heat until it just begins to smoke, about 8 minutes. Arrange paper towels nearby for draining. Test the oil by breaking off a small piece of rice stick and dropping it in. If it puffs immediately, the oil is ready. If it sinks, wait a few minutes and test again.

6] Add the rice sticks to the oil in small batches. As soon as they turn white and puffy and stop crackling, turn them and cook on the other side, about 10 seconds altogether. Immediately transfer with tongs or bamboo strainer to towels to drain. Carefully dispose of the hot oil (do not pour down the sink), leaving about 2 tablespoons in the pan. Return to high heat.

7] Add the chicken and garlic and stir-fry until the chicken is opaque, about a minute. Transfer to a platter.

8] Heat the remaining tablespoon of oil. Stir-fry the vegetables for 20 seconds. Immediately pour in the sauce and the reserved chicken. Stir and toss to combine and remove from heat.

9] Crush the cooled rice sticks by enclosing in paper towels and crunching. On a serving platter, mound the chicken mixture on half the platter and pile the rice sticks alongside. To eat, spoon the chicken filling in the center of a lettuce leaf and sprinkle with rice sticks. Roll like a soft taco and eat with fingers.

CHICKEN WITH CORN AND WILD MUSHROOMS

Here is an exceptionally light, clear version of moo goo gai pan.

✻ *Serves 4*

¾ pound boneless, skinless
  chicken breast

MARINADE
½ egg white
1 teaspoon cornstarch
½ teaspoon sugar
¼ teaspoon salt

SAUCE
3 tablespoons chicken broth
2 teaspoons light soy sauce
1 teaspoon dry sherry
¼ teaspoon sugar

1 tablespoon cornstarch mixed
  with 1 tablespoon water
2 ears fresh corn, husks removed
4 ounces fresh oyster mushrooms
2 ounces dried Chinese black
  mushrooms, soaked in hot
  water 15 minutes
4 tablespoons peanut oil
2 garlic cloves, peeled and minced
3 scallions, white and green,
  roughly chopped
¼ cup diced ham for garnish
  (optional)

1] Cut the chicken into ½-inch cubes and place in a mixing bowl. Add the marinade, toss well, and chill while continuing.

2] Combine the sauce ingredients in a small mixing bowl. Combine the cornstarch and water and set aside.

3] Remove the corn kernels by holding the cobs upright on a counter and running a sharp blade along the cobs from top to bottom.

4] Tear the fresh oyster mushrooms into bite-sized pieces, removing any tough stems. Drain and cut the rehydrated mushrooms into quarters and remove the stems. Have all of the vegetables, seasonings, and sauce ingredients ready near the stove.

5] Heat the wok over high heat. Swirl in 2 tablespoons of the peanut oil. Stir-fry the chicken until just opaque, about 2 minutes. Transfer to a platter.

6] Heat the remaining 2 tablespoons of oil over high heat. Cook the garlic and scallions until their aroma is released, 10 seconds. Add the two kinds of mushrooms and the corn and stir-fry 30 seconds. Pour in the sauce, toss well, and then add the chicken. Stir-fry, vigorously combining the ingredients, 1 to 2 minutes. Drizzle in the cornstarch mixture, stirring constantly for about a minute. Tip onto a serving platter and sprinkle with the ham garnish if desired. Serve hot.

STEAMED CHICKEN WITH CHINESE SAUSAGE

This home-style dish comes from Betty Lew of Silver Lake, California. For an easy week-night meal, you can assemble it in the morning, keep it in the refrigerator, and then steam it at dinnertime. Serve on a bed of white rice to soak up the gravy. ✕ *Serves 4*

2 skinless, boneless chicken breast
  halves

MARINADE

1 teaspoon minced garlic
1 teaspoon minced fresh ginger
2 tablespoons light soy sauce
2 tablespoons dry sherry
1 teaspoon oyster sauce
¼ teaspoon white pepper
1 tablespoon cornstarch

5 dried Chinese black mushrooms,
  soaked in hot water 15 minutes
2 lop cheung or Chinese sweet
  sausage
10 ounces (6 cups) spinach leaves,
  washed well
2 scallions, white and green, sliced

1] Cut the chicken into strips about 3 inches long by ½ inch wide. Mix the marinade ingredients together in a bowl, add the chicken, and set aside at room temperature for 20 minutes.

2] After soaking the mushrooms, drain, remove and discard the tough stems, and thinly slice the caps. Thinly slice sausages on the diagonal.

3] Bring a saucepan of water to a boil. Stir in spinach and cook just until wilted, about 20 seconds. Drain in a colander and rinse with cold water to stop the cooking. Squeeze out excess water.

4] Cover the bottom of a medium-sized heatproof ceramic bowl with the spinach. Lift the chicken pieces out of the marinade and layer over the spinach. Place the mushrooms on top of the chicken and then cover with a layer of sausage strips in a spoke pattern. Pour on the marinade. The dish can now be covered with plastic wrap and reserved in the refrigerator for several hours.

5] To steam, fill a wok with water to 1 inch below the steamer rack. Bring to a boil, reduce to a simmer, and place the prepared dish on rack. Cover and cook ½ hour. Let sit with the cover on an additional 10 minutes. Sprinkle with sliced scallions and serve hot.

PAN-FRIED SESAME CHICKEN WITH LEMON SAUCE

Chicken breasts are lightly breaded and then pan-fried to reduce the calories in classic lemon chicken. While it may be tempting to reduce the sugar in the sauce, remember that sugar accentuates the tartness of lemon. ✖ *Serves 4*

SAUCE
¼ cup chicken stock
6 tablespoons fresh lemon juice
3 tablespoons sugar
2 teaspoons grated lemon zest
2 teaspoons plum sauce

¾ cup all-purpose flour
2 eggs, beaten
½ cup white sesame seeds
2 teaspoons salt

1 teaspoon ground white pepper
4 skinless, boneless chicken breast
  halves
6 tablespoons peanut oil
1 tablespoon minced fresh ginger
1 teaspoon minced garlic
1 tablespoon cornstarch mixed
  with 1½ tablespoons water
Sliced scallion greens for garnish
  (optional)

1] Combine the sauce ingredients in a bowl and reserve.

2] To prepare the breading, place ¼ cup of the flour in a large shallow bowl or plate. In another bowl, beat the eggs, and in a third, combine the remaining ½ cup of flour with sesame seeds and salt and pepper. Arrange these next to each other on a counter.

3] Wash the chicken breasts and trim any excess fat. Pound with a mallet or rolling pin to ¼-inch thickness. Then dip, one at a time, first in the flour. Pat off any excess and dip in the egg. Lift the meat, allowing excess egg to drain back into bowl, and then dip and coat with the flour and sesame seed batter. Reserve on a platter.

4] Heat 4 tablespoons of the peanut oil in a 10-inch skillet over medium-high heat. Fry the chicken breasts, two at a time, until golden, 3 to 4 minutes per side. (Reduce the heat to medium if the chicken is browning too quickly.) Reserve on a platter.

5] While the last batch is finishing, heat the remaining 2 tablespoons of oil in a small skillet over medium heat. Sauté the ginger and garlic until their aroma is released and then pour in the sauce. When it comes to a boil, reduce to lowest heat. Drizzle in the cornstarch mixture while stirring constantly, and remove from heat as soon as the sauce thickens.

6] To serve, slice each chicken breast into ½-inch strips along the width and place on dinner plates. Spoon on the sauce and garnish with scallions, if desired.

CHICKEN WITH WALNUTS

Cubed chicken with nuts is considered a special-occasion dish in China. ✕ *Serves 4*

¾ pound skinless, boneless
  chicken breast

MARINADE
½ egg white
1 teaspoon oyster sauce
½ teaspoon salt
¼ teaspoon white pepper

1 cup plus 3 tablespoons peanut
  oil
1 cup walnut halves
1 teaspoon minced garlic
1 teaspoon minced fresh ginger
1 tablespoon soy sauce
1 tablespoon dry sherry
1 teaspoon sesame oil
½ teaspoon sugar

1] Trim the chicken of any fat and cut into ½-inch cubes. Place in a bowl with the marinade ingredients. Mix well and set aside while preparing the other ingredients.

2] Heat 1 cup of the peanut oil in a wok or deep saucepan to deep-fry temperature, about 5 minutes. Fry the walnuts until golden but not dark brown, less than a minute. Transfer with a slotted spoon to paper towels to drain. Carefully pour off the oil and wipe the wok clean with paper towels.

3] Heat the wok over high heat and then add 2 tablespoons of the oil. Stir-fry the chicken until it just loses its pink color, about 1 minute, and push to the sides of the wok.

4] Pour the remaining 1 tablespoon peanut oil in the center. Briefly stir-fry the garlic and ginger and then add the soy sauce, sherry, sesame oil, and sugar. Stir to combine the sauce, seasonings, and chicken over high heat for about a minute. Add the fried walnuts and toss just to combine. Serve hot.

KUNG PAU CHICKEN

—————■—————

It helps to know your diners when preparing this restaurant favorite. You can control the heat by adjusting the number of dried red chile peppers to taste—4 for moderate heat, 8 for mouth on fire for the rest of the meal. ✕ *Serves 4*

¾ pound skinless, boneless
   chicken breast

MARINADE———————————
1 tablespoon dry sherry
2 teaspoons soy sauce
1 teaspoon sesame oil
1 tablespoon cornstarch

—————————————————————

1 tablespoon minced fresh ginger
1 tablespoon minced garlic
4 to 8 dried red chile peppers,
   roughly chopped with seeds
1 green bell pepper, seeded and
   cut in ½-inch cubes
3 scallions, white and green, cut
   in ½-inch lengths on the
   diagonal

SAUCE————————————————
2 tablespoons soy sauce
1 tablespoon dry sherry
2 teaspoons Chinese black vinegar
2 teaspoons sesame oil
½ teaspoon sugar
½ teaspoon Chinese chili sauce
½ teaspoon Szechuan
   peppercorns, roasted and
   ground

—————————————————————

2 teaspoons cornstarch mixed with
   2 teaspoons water
1 cup plus 1 tablespoon peanut oil
1 cup whole raw cashews

1] Cut the chicken into ½-inch cubes. Place in a mixing bowl with sherry, soy, and sesame oil. Toss well, add the cornstarch, and mix again. Refrigerate while preparing the other ingredients.

2] Place all the chopped ingredients on a platter near the stove. Mix the sauce ingredients in a bowl. Prepare the cornstarch mixture.

3] Heat 1 cup of the peanut oil in a wok to deep-fry temperature. Line nearby counters with paper towels for draining.

4] Cook the cashews, stirring frequently, just until golden, about 10 seconds. With a slotted spoon quickly transfer to paper towels to drain.

5] Pour off all but 2 tablespoons of the oil in the wok and return it to high heat. Stir-fry the chicken until it loses its pink color. Transfer to a platter with a slotted spoon.

6] Add the remaining tablespoon of peanut oil to the hot wok. Stir-fry the ginger, garlic, and dried red chile peppers until their aroma is released, less than a minute. Add the bell pepper and scallions and continue stir-frying about 20 seconds.

7] Pour in the liquid sauce ingredients, followed by the chicken and cashews. Stir well to combine ingredients. Then, with the heat still high, drizzle in the cornstarch and water, stirring constantly to thicken and coat evenly. Serve hot.

CHICKEN WITH GARLIC AND BLACK BEANS

This quick family-style dish is perfect for weeknight cooking.
Serves 4

3½ pounds chicken fryer parts
2 tablespoons salted black beans, finely chopped
1 tablespoon minced fresh ginger
3 tablespoons minced garlic (1 small head)

¼ cup peanut oil
2 tablespoons soy sauce
¼ cup chicken stock

1] Wash the chicken and pat dry. Leaving the skin and bones intact, chop into large bite-sized pieces. The key to chopping through bones is to use your heaviest, sharpest knife, preferably a cleaver. Instead of sawing back and forth, hold the knife solely at its handle and raise it at a 45-degree angle. Let the blade fall with a loose flick of the wrist, so the full weight of the blade hits the bone cleanly and sharply. It should only take a few whacks at each spot to cut through. Of course, you should first take the bird apart at the joints.

2] Combine the chopped black beans, ginger, and garlic in a small bowl.

3] Heat a wok over high heat. Swirl in the peanut oil and stir-fry the black bean mixture for 10 seconds. Add the chicken and stir-fry until it is golden all over, about 5 minutes.

4] Pour in the soy sauce and chicken stock. Reduce the heat to low and cook, uncovered, 15 minutes. Stir the meat occasionally to ensure even cooking. With a slotted spoon, transfer chicken pieces to a serving platter and serve hot.

ROASTED SZECHUAN DUCK WITH HONEY GINGER GLAZE

━━━━━■━━━━━

This easy preparation yields an exceptionally succulent bird—brown and crisp on the outside and fragrant with a gentle combination of sweet, spicy, and salty within. If you have not cooked duck before, do not be intimidated. It is no more difficult than cooking a chicken.

Ducks are available, frozen, at specialty shops and some supermarkets. They take a day to defrost in the refrigerator. Roasted duck makes a lovely special dinner for two, served with stir-fried Snow Peas and Water Chestnuts (see page 96). ✖ *Serves 2*

One 4-pound duckling
Soy sauce
1 tablespoon coarse salt
1 teaspoon roasted and ground
    Szechuan peppercorns (see page
    16)
½ teaspoon five-spice powder
One 2-inch piece peeled ginger
½ orange, cut in half

GLAZE
Juice of ½ orange
¼ cup honey
1 tablespoon minced fresh ginger
2 teaspoons hoisin sauce
1 teaspoon sesame oil
1 teaspoon soy sauce

orange slices for garnish (optional)

1] Wash the duck in cold water, removing neck and giblets from cavity. Pat dry. Trim any excess fat and skin. Rub the duck inside and out with soy sauce.

2] Place the salt in a small skillet and roast over medium heat until lightly browned, about 5 minutes. In a small dish, combine the roasted salt with Szechuan peppercorns and five spice powder. Rub the duck inside and out with the spice mixture. Stuff the cavity with the piece of ginger and the orange quarters. Let sit at room temperature 1 hour for the flavors to penetrate. Before roasting, puncture duck breast and legs several times with a skewer or tip of a sharp blade, to allow the fat to drain while cooking.

3] Preheat oven to 450 F. Place a rack in a shallow roasting pan and pour water beneath the rack to prevent splattering and keep the bird moist. Place duck on the rack, breast side up, and roast, uncovered, 20 minutes. Then reduce heat to 350 F and roast another 45 minutes.

4] A few minutes before roasting time is up, combine the glaze ingredients in a small saucepan. Cook over medium-low heat, stirring to dissolve the honey, about 2 minutes. Brush liberally over the duck breast and legs and put back in the oven for 5 minutes more. Then remove and brush again with remaining glaze. Return to the oven for another 5 minutes. Transfer duck to a cutting board to cool for 10 minutes.

5] To serve, remove the legs at the joint. Slice each half breast off the bone, keeping the meat and skin intact. Then slice the breast meat into ½-inch slices across the grain. Place a leg and breast on each dinner plate and garnish with orange slices, if desired.

BEEF AND BROCCOLI IN OYSTER SAUCE

Pungent oyster sauce is the classic complement to beef and broccoli, whether alone or together. This is wonderful served over Crisp Noodle Pancake (see page 89). ✗ *Serves 4*

¾ pound flank steak
MARINADE_____
1 tablespoon soy sauce
2 teaspoons dry sherry
2 teaspoons cornstarch
_____
1 large stalk broccoli, about
   10 ounces
2 tablespoons oyster sauce
1 tablespoon soy sauce

1 tablespoon dry sherry
1 tablespoon water
¼ teaspoon sugar
2 teaspoons cornstarch mixed with
   4 teaspoons water
3 tablespoons peanut oil
1 tablespoon minced garlic
2 tablespoons minced scallions,
   white and green

1] Slice the steak first into ¼-inch-wide strips across the grain. Then cut the strips into 1-inch lengths. Place in a medium mixing bowl. Combine with the marinade ingredients and refrigerate.

2] Trim and discard the bottom 2 inches of broccoli stem. Cut into individual florets with long, thin stems. Bring a medium saucepan of salted water to a boil. Cook the broccoli just until the water returns to a rapid boil. Drain in a colander, rinse with cold water, and reserve.

3] Meanwhile combine the oyster sauce, soy sauce, dry sherry, water, and sugar in a small bowl. Mix together the cornstarch and water.

4] Place the wok over high heat and swirl in 2 tablespoons of the peanut oil. Stir-fry the beef until it loses its red color, about 2 minutes. Transfer to a platter.

5] Return the wok to high heat; swirl in the remaining tablespoon of oil. Stir-fry the garlic and scallions just until their aroma is released, about 10 seconds. Add the blanched broccoli and toss to heat through and coat with oil, about 30 seconds. Then pour in the sauce and beef. Toss well and cook an additional minute. Drizzle in the cornstarch mixture, stirring constantly to thicken, about 30 seconds. Remove from heat and serve.

BEEF WITH ONIONS
AND PEPPERS

This standard restaurant dish plays the rich, hearty flavor of beef against crisp, crunchy peppers and onions. Adjust the spicy Chinese chili sauce in the sauce to taste. ✖ *Serves 4*

¾ pound flank steak, cut into
  ½-inch cubes

MARINADE_____
2 teaspoons soy sauce
2 teaspoons sesame oil
2 teaspoons cornstarch

3 garlic cloves, peeled and minced
1 teaspoon minced fresh ginger
1 onion, peeled and cut in eighths
2 bell peppers, green, red, or
  yellow, cored, seeded, and cut
  in ½-inch cubes

SAUCE_____
2 tablespoons soy sauce
1 tablespoon dry sherry
½ teaspoon sugar
½ teaspoon Chinese chili sauce
1 teaspoon sesame oil

4 tablespoons corn oil or peanut
  oil

1] Place the beef in a bowl, add the marinade ingredients, and toss well. Marinate in the refrigerator for 1 hour. Meanwhile, prepare all the vegetables and combine the sauce ingredients in a small bowl.

2] Heat the wok over high heat. Heat 2 tablespoons of the oil and add the beef. Stir-fry until it just loses its redness, about 3 minutes. Spoon into a strainer set over a bowl, to drain the meat of excess fat and oil.

3] Heat the remaining 2 tablespoons of oil in the wok. Stir-fry the garlic and ginger until their aroma is released, 10 seconds. Add the onion and peppers and stir-fry 1½ minutes, breaking up the onion layers as you stir and toss. Return the beef to the wok, pour in the sauce, and stir-fry an additional 2 minutes. Remove from heat and serve.

BOK CHOY BEEF

In this homey dish, the beef plays a secondary role to bright, crunchy bok choy. ✖ *Serves 4*

½ pound flank steak, sliced paper-thin across the grain

MARINADE_____
1 teaspoon soy sauce
1 teaspoon peanut oil
1 teaspoon cornstarch
_____

1 large bunch bok choy, washed and cut into 1-inch slices across the width
5 dried Chinese black mushrooms, soaked in hot water 15 minutes

SAUCE_____
1 tablespoon soy sauce
2 teaspoons dry sherry
1 teaspoon oyster sauce
1 teaspoon sesame oil
_____

1 tablespoon cornstarch mixed with 1 tablespoon water
3 tablespoons corn oil or peanut oil
2 large garlic cloves, peeled and slivered
Salt

1] Place the thinly shredded beef in a bowl. Toss with the marinade ingredients and refrigerate for 1½ hours.

2] Bring a large saucepan of salted water to a boil. Blanch the bok choy just until the water returns to a rapid boil. Drain and rinse with cold water. Pat dry with paper towels.

3] Drain the mushrooms, discard the stems, and slice thinly. Combine the sauce ingredients in a small bowl and the cornstarch mixture in another. Arrange near the stove.

4] Heat the wok over high heat. Swirl in 1 tablespoon of the corn or peanut oil. Add the blanched bok choy, garlic, and a pinch of salt. Stir and toss until the bok choy is bright green and coated with oil. Transfer to a bowl.

5] Add the remaining 2 tablespoons of the oil to the hot wok. Stir-fry the beef until it loses its redness, about 3 minutes. Add the mushrooms, stir and toss 10 seconds, and then add the bok choy and sauce. Cook an additional 20 seconds with the heat high. Drizzle in the cornstarch mixture, stirring constantly for 1 minute more, and remove from heat. Serve immediately over bowls of rice for the gravy.

ORANGE-SCENTED BEEF

The tartness of orange balances beef's rich flavor. Here is an elegant main course to serve with Cold Tossed Asparagus with Sesame Seeds (see page 95) and, for a cross-cultural touch, some crusty French bread.
✖ *Serves 4*

1 pound flank steak

MARINADE_____
1 tablespoon soy sauce
2 teaspoons dry sherry
1 tablespoon peanut oil
½ teaspoon sugar
1 tablespoon cornstarch

_____

2 pieces dried orange peel, or
   1 tablespoon grated orange zest
2 teaspoons minced fresh ginger

SAUCE_____
2 tablespoons fresh orange juice
1 tablespoon soy sauce
1 teaspoon rice wine vinegar
2 teaspoons sugar

_____

3 tablespoons peanut oil

1] Cut the flank steak in half along the grain. Then thinly slice across the grain. Transfer to a mixing bowl. Toss with the marinade ingredients, cover, and reserve in the refrigerator at least 1 hour, or as long as a day.

2] Soak the 2 pieces of dried orange peel in hot tap water for 15 minutes to soften. Then mince, measure out 1 tablespoon, and reserve with the minced ginger.

3] Combine the sauce ingredients in a small bowl and place near the stove.

4] Place the wok over high heat. Swirl in 2 tablespoons of the oil. Stir-fry the beef until it just loses its red color, about a minute. Spoon the beef into a strainer and place on a bowl to drain. Return the wok to high heat.

5] Add the remaining 1 tablespoon of oil. Briefly stir-fry the ginger and orange peel, about 10 seconds. Then return the beef to the wok along with the sauce. Stir and toss 30 seconds just to combine, and serve.

MU SHU PORK WITH TORTILLA PANCAKES

This is one of those dishes that actually tastes better at home than in most restaurants, where cooks often must use inferior ingredients to keep costs down. The only thing that takes any time is shredding the pork, and if you live near a Chinatown, you can eliminate that by purchasing precut and shredded pork ready for stir-frying. *✗ Serves 4*

¾ pound boneless pork butt or
   loin, thinly sliced and julienned

MARINADE_____
2 tablespoons light soy sauce
1 tablespoon dry sherry
1 teaspoon hoisin sauce

_____
1 ounce bean threads
2 large dried tree ear mushrooms
3 ribs (1½ cups thinly sliced) bok
   choy
3 scallions, white and green, cut
   in 2-inch lengths and slivered
2 cups thinly sliced Napa cabbage

2 eggs
¼ teaspoon salt

SAUCE_____
2 tablespoons chicken stock
1 tablespoon light soy sauce
½ tablespoon dry sherry
½ teaspoon sugar
¼ teaspoon salt

_____
4 tablespoons peanut oil
Sesame oil
8 flour tortillas
Hoisin sauce

1] Place the slivered pork in a mixing bowl. Add the marinade ingredients and toss to coat. Set aside at room temperature for 20 minutes.

2] Reconstitute the bean threads and mushrooms in separate bowls of hot water for 15 minutes. Then drain and roughly chop the bean threads into 2-inch lengths. Squeeze excess water out of the tree ear mushrooms, trim the tough spots, and thinly slice. Place on a platter with the bok choy, scallions, and cabbage.

3] Lightly beat the eggs and salt with a fork. Combine the sauce ingredients in a small bowl. Have everything ready near the stove.

4] Place the wok over high heat. Swirl in 1 tablespoon of the peanut oil. Pour in the eggs and swirl and turn the wok so the eggs form a thin puffy film, about 1 minute. While eggs are still runny, transfer to a platter and break into bite-sized pieces.

5] Return the wok to high heat and swirl in 2 more tablespoons of the oil. Stir-fry the pork just until it loses its pinkness, about a minute. Transfer to the platter with the eggs.

6] Add the remaining tablespoon of oil to the wok. Add the bean threads and all the vegetables and stir-fry 1 minute, until the bok choy brightens.

7] Pour in the sauce, stir to combine, and then return the pork and scrambled eggs to the wok. Cook half a minute more and sprinkle lightly with sesame oil. Tip onto a platter and cover to keep warm.

8] Wrap the tortillas in aluminum foil and warm in a 350 F oven for 15 minutes. To serve, lightly coat a tortilla with hoisin sauce. Spoon about ½ cup of mu shu mixture in the center, roll into a cylinder, and fold up ends to enclose. Serve with chopsticks or forks for stray bits—this is a messy dish.

BARBECUED PORK

Traditionally flavored Chinese barbecued meats are easy to prepare at home without special equipment. All you need is a roasting pan and rack. Leftovers have many uses, from a garnish for won ton soup, fried rice, or lo mein to American barbecued pork sandwiches. ✻ *Serves 6*

3 pounds boneless pork butt,
    trimmed of excess fat

MARINADE_____

¼ cup soy sauce
2 tablespoons dry sherry
2 tablespoons hoisin sauce
2 tablespoons ground bean sauce

1 tablespoon honey
1 tablespoon sugar
3 garlic cloves, peeled and crushed
1 teaspoon five-spice powder

GLAZE_____

2 tablespoons honey
2 tablespoons sesame oil

1] Slice the pork into about 12 strips about 4 inches long by 2 inches wide. Place in a shallow glass or ceramic dish.

2] Mix the marinade ingredients in a bowl and then pour over the meat. Rub marinade all over meat. Cover with plastic wrap and let sit at room temperature 3 hours. Turn the pieces and rub with marinade after 1½ hours.

3] Preheat the oven to 350 F. Arrange a rack in a large roasting pan and cover the bottom with ¼ inch of water. Wipe off excess marinade and arrange pork on rack, being careful that the meat does not touch the water. (The purpose of the water is to catch splatters and make cleanup easier, not to braise the meat.) Bake 50 minutes.

4] Remove from oven and turn up the heat to 400 F. Mix the glaze in a small bowl. Brush tops of the pork strips with glaze and bake 5 minutes more. Using tongs, turn the strips over, brush with glaze, and return to the oven for the final 5 minutes. Set aside for 10 minutes before slicing across the grain into ⅛-inch slices.

MA PO TOFU

If tofu has always seemed like bland health food to you, this dish could change your mind. A favorite Chinese family dish, it incorporates the fire and spice of western China with inexpensive tofu and ground pork for a soul-satisfying dish. ✖ *Serves 4*

One 14-ounce package firm tofu, drained

SAUCE————————————
½ cup chicken stock
2 tablespoons dry sherry
2 tablespoons soy sauce
2 teaspoons ground bean sauce
1 teaspoon sesame oil
½ teaspoon Chinese chili sauce
½ teaspoon sugar
¼ teaspoon roasted and ground Szechuan peppercorns, or black pepper
¼ teaspoon salt

1 tablespoon peanut oil
4 garlic cloves, peeled and minced
4 scallions, white and green, minced
1 tablespoon minced fresh ginger
½ pound ground pork
¼ cup chopped cilantro for garnish

1] Cut the tofu into ½-inch cubes and reserve. Combine all of the sauce ingredients in a bowl.

2] Heat a wok over high heat. Swirl in peanut oil. Stir-fry the garlic, scallions, and ginger until their aromas are released, about 30 seconds. Add the pork, stir, and toss until it just loses its pink color, about 2 minutes. Pour in the sauce and cook over high heat 5 minutes.

3] Stir in the tofu to combine. Reduce heat to medium-low and cook, stirring occasionally, 10 minutes, uncovered. When done the mixture should have the consistency of a moist stew, not a soup. Serve in bowls, sprinkled with cilantro.

Chinese Cooking for Beginners

STIR-FRY PORK WITH LONG BEANS

I love the simplicity of stir-fry dishes that match a meat with a single vegetable. Feel free to experiment with substitutions: chicken or shrimp for the pork and perhaps broccoli or scallions for the long beans, according to your taste. A good stir-fry should not be a jumble of too many flavors. ✖ *Serves 4*

¾ pound pork loin

MARINADE

2 teaspoons light soy sauce
2 teaspoons dry sherry
1 teaspoon cornstarch

¾ pound green beans or Chinese long beans, trimmed and cut in 1-inch lengths

SAUCE

3 tablespoons chicken stock or water

1 tablespoon hoisin sauce
1 tablespoon dry sherry
2 teaspoons soy sauce

2 teaspoons cornstarch mixed with 1 tablespoon water
6 Chinese dried black mushrooms, soaked in hot water 15 minutes
4 tablespoons peanut oil or corn oil
2 teaspoons minced fresh ginger
2 teaspoons minced garlic

1] Trim the pork of excess fat and sinew and cut into ½-inch cubes. Place in a mixing bowl, toss with the marinade ingredients, and reserve in the refrigerator.

2] Bring a large saucepan of salted water to a boil. Cook the green beans 2 minutes after the water returns to a boil. Drain, rinse with cold water, and reserve.

3] Combine the sauce ingredients in a small bowl. Prepare the cornstarch mixture in another bowl. Trim the stems off the reconstituted mushrooms and thinly slice the caps. Have all the ingredients ready near the stove.

4] Heat the wok over high heat. Add 2 tablespoons of the peanut oil and stir-fry the pork just until it loses its pink color, 2 minutes. Transfer to a platter.

5] Swirl in the remaining 2 tablespoons of oil. Cook the ginger and garlic about 10 seconds and then add the blanched green beans and mushrooms. Stir-fry 1 minute. Pour in the sauce and the pork and toss well. Over high heat, drizzle in the cornstarch mixture, stirring constantly until it thickens and coats the food. Remove from heat and serve.

SWEET AND SOUR PORK

This Chinese-American restaurant favorite is virtually unknown in China, where fish is considered the proper complement to sweet and sour sauce. The addition of canned fruits like pineapple in such a dish would be considered barbaric. This version, however, remains true to the 1950s restaurant dish—ketchup and all. ✂ *Serves 4*

1 pound pork tenderloin
MARINADE
1 egg yolk
1 tablespoon soy sauce
1 tablespoon cornstarch

1 red bell pepper, cored and seeded
1 green pepper, cored and seeded
4 scallions, white and green, cut in ½-inch lengths

SAUCE
½ cup water or chicken stock
3 tablespoons ketchup
2 tablespoons distilled white vinegar
2 tablespoons sugar
½ teaspoon salt

1 tablespoon cornstarch mixed with 2 tablespoons water
3 cups plus 1 tablespoon peanut or corn oil
¾ cup cornstarch

1] Cut the pork into 1-inch cubes. Beat the egg yolk and soy sauce together in a bowl. Add the pork, toss well, and add the 1 tablespoon cornstarch. Stir to combine and set aside.

2] Meanwhile cut the peppers into ½-inch squares. Set aside with the scallions. Combine the sauce ingredients in a bowl and prepare the cornstarch and water mixture in another small bowl.

3] Heat 3 cups of the oil in a wok over high heat to deep-fry temperature, 350 degrees. While the oil is heating, place the ¾ cup of cornstarch in a bowl. Lift the pork out of the marinade and add to the cornstarch. Toss the pork so it is well coated with batter and let sit in the cornstarch while the oil heats.

4] Test oil by dropping in a piece of pork. If bubbles form and the crust turns brown within seconds the oil is ready. Line the counters with paper towels for draining. Fry the pork in batches, patting off excess cornstarch before plunging in oil. Cooking time is about 2 minutes per batch, or until the batter is crisp and golden brown. Remove with slotted spoon or strainer and drain on paper towels.

5] Carefully pour off the hot oil. Return the wok to high heat and swirl in the remaining tablespoon of oil. Stir-fry the scallions and peppers for 1 minute. Pour in the sauce, stir well, and then add the pork. Stir-fry over high heat 1 minute more. With the sauce at a boil, drizzle in the cornstarch and water mixture, stirring constantly. Stir until the sauce thickens and clings to the meat, about 1 minute. Remove from heat and serve.

PEKING LAMB STEW

Northern Chinese cooking is not well represented in this country, where most restaurant cooking is either from southern Canton or western Szechuan. This robust stew is characteristic of the north, where the winters are cold and the cooking hearty. Like all stews, this one can be made well in advance and reheated. ✖ *Serves 6*

3 pounds lamb shoulder meat
Salt and white pepper
2 whites of leeks, cut in half and
    washed
2 carrots, peeled
½ cup corn oil
1 tablespoon minced fresh ginger

1 tablespoon minced garlic
¾ teaspoon black pepper
½ teaspoon salt
4½ cups Chinese Chicken Stock
    (see page 23) or canned stock
2 tablespoons hoisin sauce
1 star anise

1] Trim the meat of excess fat and bone. Cut into 2-inch cubes. Sprinkle with salt and white pepper.

2] Dice the leeks and carrots.

3] Heat the oil in a large dutch oven over high heat. Cook the lamb in batches until golden brown all over. Remove to a platter.

4] Add the leeks and carrots to the oil in the pan and cook over high heat until nearly golden, about 5 minutes. Reduce the heat to medium, add the ginger, garlic, black pepper, and salt, and cook, stirring frequently, about 3 minutes.

5] Return the meat to the pan. Pour in the chicken stock and remaining ingredients. Bring to a boil, reduce to a simmer, and cook, uncovered, 1 hour. Occasionally skim and discard the fat and foam that rise.

6] Cook an additional ½ hour with cover on to further condense the stock and soften the meat. The meat should be tender and the stock quite concentrated when done. Serve over rice.

BRAISED RED SNAPPER IN SOY SAUCE

A wonderful dish to serve buffet-style, since it is also delicious at room temperature. ✂ *Serves 4*

One 2½-pound red snapper or
   rock cod, cleaned and scaled,
   with head and tail left on
¼ cup all-purpose flour
Salt and pepper

SAUCE ————————————
¾ cup chicken stock
½ cup dry sherry
¼ cup soy sauce
1 teaspoon sugar

1 star anise
¼ teaspoon black pepper

————————————
¼ cup peanut oil
1 garlic clove, peeled and crushed
3 scallions, white and green, cut
   in 2-inch lengths and slivered,
   for garnish

1] Wash the fish and pat dry. Lightly dust with flour and sprinkle with salt and pepper. Score diagonally 2 or 3 times on each side with a sharp cleaver.

2] Combine the sauce ingredients in a bowl and pour into a wok. Bring to a boil and reduce to a simmer.

3] Meanwhile place your largest skillet over high heat and then add the peanut oil. Toss the garlic in the oil until the aroma is released and then remove and discard. Pan-fry the fish until crisp and brown, about 3 minutes per side. Reduce the heat if the oil is burning.

4] With a spatula and a serving spoon transfer the fish to the wok with simmering sauce. Cover and cook 4 minutes per side. Transfer the fish to a large serving platter.

5] Turn the heat up to high and boil the sauce, uncovered, 3 minutes more to concentrate the flavors. Strain over the fish on the platter. Garnish with scallions and serve hot or at room temperature.

STEAMED WHOLE FISH WITH GINGER AND SCALLIONS

There is no better way to eat fresh, whole fish than this classic Cantonese preparation. If you cannot get to a Chinese market, where knowledgeable customers and high demand assure the best fish, do shop at a busy fish market rather than the supermarket.

Look for clear eyes, bright red blood in the gills and inside the stomach, and a clean, fresh smell. Fresh fish does not smell fishy. Always purchase fish on the same day you plan to cook it, and store it in the refrigerator. ✖ *Serves 4*

2 garlic cloves, peeled and crushed
2 thick fresh ginger slices, unpeeled and crushed
2 scallions, white and green, cut in 2-inch lengths
One 2-pound red snapper or rock cod, cleaned and scaled, with head and tail left on

2 tablespoons (about 1½ inches) peeled and slivered ginger
¼ cup peanut oil
1 tablespoon sesame oil
1 tablespoon light soy sauce
2 or 3 scallions, cut in 2-inch lengths and slivered

1] Fill a wok or steamer with water to within an inch of the steamer rack. Bring to a boil, reduce to a simmer, and add the garlic, unpeeled ginger slices, and scallion slices to the water.

2] Prepare the fish by cutting 3 deep gashes along the width on each side so the flavors penetrate the meat. Stuff the slivered ginger in the gashes. Lightly coat the plate for steaming with peanut oil and place the fish on it. Place on steaming rack. Cover and steam over low heat for 20 to 25 minutes.

3] About 5 minutes before the fish is done, combine the ¼ cup peanut oil and the sesame oil in a small pan and place over moderate heat until hot, about 5 minutes. Remove from heat and stir in the soy sauce, which will sizzle. Have the slivered scallions ready nearby.

4] Test the fish for doneness by poking with a chopstick at its thickest point. If the meat easily pulls away from the bones, it is done. With a spatula or a serving spoon on either end, transfer fish to a serving platter. Scatter the slivered scallions all over, drizzle with the hot oil, and serve immediately.

MONKFISH WITH SIZZLING CHILI OIL

Tender, moist fish fillets are enhanced by a drizzle of flavored oil. This simple fish preparation was inspired by Martin Yan, the television chef. ✖ *Serves 4*

2 tablespoons dry sherry
2 tablespoons light soy sauce

SIZZLING CHILI OIL————————
½ cup peanut oil
2 scallions, white and green, cut
   in 2-inch lengths and slivered
2 inches peeled ginger, slivered
2 teaspoons minced garlic
2 dried red chile peppers, cut in
   ½-inch lengths

2 teaspoons sesame oil
¼ teaspoon salt
2 tablespoons light soy sauce

————————————————

3 slices unpeeled ginger, crushed
2 scallions, cut in 2-inch lengths
Four 6-ounce monkfish fillets

1] Combine the dry sherry and soy sauce and rub all over the fish fillets. Assemble the sizzling chili oil ingredients.

2] If using a wok, coat a plate with peanut oil and place over rack for steaming. Pour in water to within an inch of the rack. Add the unpeeled ginger and scallions to the water, bring to a boil, and reduce to a simmer. Place the fish on plate, cover, and cook for 10 to 14 minutes, depending on thickness. To test, poke thickest part with a chopstick. If the center is opaque, the fish is done.

3] A few minutes before the fish is done, warm the peanut oil in a small saucepan over moderate heat until hot, 3 minutes. Stir in the slivered scallions and ginger, garlic, red chile peppers, sesame oil, and salt and cook 30 seconds. Remove from heat and stir in the soy sauce.

4] With a spatula, transfer the finished fish to serving plates. Drizzle with hot oil mixture and serve.

STEAMED CATFISH WITH BLACK BEANS

━━━━━━━━■━━━━━━━━

The full flavor of catfish makes it an excellent vehicle for pungent black beans. Serve with a bowl of rice and fresh greens to offset the richness. (Now that most catfish is farm-raised, it no longer deserves its unsavory reputation as a scavenger.) ✕ *Serves 4*

Four 6-ounce catfish fillets
Peanut oil
1 tablespoon salted black beans
2 tablespoons thinly sliced
    scallions

2 teaspoons minced garlic
2 teaspoons minced fresh ginger
2 tablespoons light soy sauce
2 tablespoons dry sherry

1] Rinse the fish with cold water and pat dry. Prepare a steamer rack over water and bring to a boil. Coat the tray or plate for steaming with peanut oil.

2] Place the black beans in a small strainer and rinse with cold water. Place in a small bowl with scallions, garlic, ginger, soy sauce, and dry sherry. Using the back of a spoon make a paste by crushing the beans and combining with other ingredients.

3] Place the fish on the steaming tray or plate, overlapping if necessary. Divide the black bean mixture into 4 portions and spoon over each fillet. Cover and steam over low heat for 10 minutes, or until the center of each fillet is opaque when poked with a chopstick. Transfer with a spatula to serving plates.

ASIAN BARBECUED
SALMON

Oily fish like salmon, swordfish, and tuna are not considered fit to eat in China, where flakier, more delicate-tasting fish such as rock cod and snapper are prized. As a Californian, however, I just couldn't resist a grilled summer fish. Salmon steaks marry well with Asian flavors and they are easy to handle on the grill or broiler. ✄ *Serves 4*

MARINADE
½ cup light soy sauce
½ cup fresh lemon juice
¼ cup plum sauce
2 tablespoons sesame oil
½ teaspoon black pepper

4 salmon steaks
Peanut oil

1] Combine the soy sauce, lemon juice, plum sauce, sesame oil, and pepper in a ceramic bowl. Add the fish, rub it all over with marinade, and let sit for ½ hour. (Because of its delicate flavor and texture, fish is always marinated for a short time, preferably in a ceramic or plastic container, so it does not pick up a metallic taste.)

2] Preheat the grill or broiler for 15 minutes. Lightly coat the grate with peanut oil to prevent sticking.

3] Cook the steaks 4 to 5 minutes per side, using a spatula to flip. Serve immediately.

SPICY TANGERINE SCALLOPS

Plump, rich sea scallops are a good foil for this sweet, spicy citrus sauce. This is a good dinner party dish—but make sure the accompaniments are made in advance since, like most stir-fry dishes, this one is best served immediately. ✕ *Serves 4*

SAUCE
¼ cup chicken stock
1 tablespoon dry sherry
1 tablespoon light soy sauce
1 teaspoon sesame oil
¼ teaspoon Chinese chili sauce
2 teaspoons sugar
1 tablespoon grated orange or
    tangerine zest
½ tablespoon salt

1 pound sea scallops
2 teaspoons minced fresh ginger
1 teaspoon minced garlic
1 large red pepper, cored, seeded,
    and cut in ½-inch cubes
2 scallions, white and green, cut
    in 1-inch lengths
1 tablespoon cornstarch mixed
    with 2 tablespoons water
3 tablespoons peanut oil

1] Combine the sauce ingredients in a bowl. Cut the scallops into quarters. Prepare all the seasonings and vegetables and arrange on a platter near the stove. Mix the cornstarch with water and keep nearby.

2] Place a wok over high heat. Swirl in 1 tablespoon of the peanut oil and stir-fry the scallops just until opaque, about 3 minutes. Transfer to a platter.

3] Swirl the remaining 2 tablespoons of oil into the wok and return to high heat. Stir-fry the ginger and garlic with red pepper and scallions about 2 minutes. Return the scallops to the wok and pour in the sauce. Toss and stir another minute and then drizzle in the cornstarch mixture, stirring constantly, for 1 minute more. Serve immediately.

SHRIMP AND ASPARAGUS

This subtle combination makes an elegant supper served with steamed rice, a green salad, and a glass of white wine. ✖ *Serves 2 to 4*

¾ pound large shrimp

MARINADE
1 tablespoon dry sherry
¼ teaspoon salt
1 teaspoon cornstarch

SAUCE
2 tablespoons dry sherry
1 teaspoon salt
½ teaspoon sugar
½ teaspoon sesame oil
¼ teaspoon white pepper

1 tablespoon cornstarch mixed
  with 1 tablespoon water

3 tablespoons peanut oil
1 large garlic clove, peeled and
  minced
½ pound asparagus, preferably
  thin, ends trimmed, cut into
  2-inch lengths
¼ cup chicken broth

1] Shell and devein the shrimp. Place in a bowl with the marinade ingredients. Mix to combine, and reserve in the refrigerator while preparing the other ingredients.

2] Combine the sauce ingredients in a small bowl and prepare the cornstarch and water mixture.

3] Heat 2 tablespoons of the oil in a wok or large skillet over high heat. Add the shrimp, lifting them out of the marinade with a slotted spoon to drain and avoid splattering. Stir-fry with the garlic just until the shrimp turns pink, about 2 minutes. Transfer to a platter.

4] Pour the remaining 1 tablespoon of oil into the hot wok. Stir-fry the asparagus for a few seconds, just to brighten. Pour in the chicken broth and cook over high heat until only about a tablespoon of liquid remains in the pan.

5] Return the shrimp to the pan and briefly toss. Pour in the sauce, toss to combine, and bring to a boil. Drizzle in the cornstarch mixture, stirring constantly for an additional minute. Serve immediately.

Chinese Cooking for Beginners

SHRIMP AND LEEKS

This delicate Cantonese dish tastes even sweeter with Chinese yellow chives rather than leeks. They are available at Chinese markets, where they are also called chives or tender shoots; if you substitute ½ pound chives, reduce simmering time by 5 minutes. ✖ *Serves 4*

1 pound large shrimp, shelled and
   deveined

MARINADE
1 tablespoon dry sherry
1½ teaspoons cornstarch

4 tablespoons peanut oil
2 teaspoons minced garlic

2 leeks, white and pale green parts
½ teaspoon salt
Dash white pepper
½ cup chicken stock
¼ teaspoon sugar
1 teaspoon sesame oil

1] Clean the shrimp and mix with the marinade ingredients in a bowl. Reserve in the refrigerator while preparing other ingredients.

2] In a large skillet, heat 2 tablespoons of the peanut oil over high heat. Lift the shrimp from the marinade with a slotted spoon to drain excess moisture. Stir-fry just until pink, about 2 minutes. Transfer to a platter.

3] Add the remaining 2 tablespoons of peanut oil to the pan. Reduce heat to medium-high and add the garlic, leeks, salt, and pepper. Stir-fry about 1 minute.

4] Pour in chicken stock and sugar. Reduce heat to low, cover, and cook 10 minutes. Remove the cover, return the shrimp to the pan, and stir to combine and heat the shrimp through. Turn off heat, drizzle on sesame oil, and serve.

CLAMS IN
BLACK BEAN SAUCE

———————————■———————————

The strong flavors of black beans, garlic, and ginger go well with tender clams. ✕ *Serves 2*

2 pounds clams, such as littleneck
2 slices fresh ginger, crushed
1 tablespoon salted black beans,
   minced
1 tablespoon minced garlic
1 tablespoon minced fresh ginger

SAUCE————————————————
½ cup chicken stock
2 tablespoons dry sherry

2 tablespoons soy sauce
1 teaspoon sugar

————————————————————————
1 tablespoon cornstarch
2 tablespoons reserved clam
   cooking liquid
3 tablespoons peanut oil

1] Scrub the clams with a brush under cold running water.

2] Pour 1 quart of cold water into a stockpot or saucepan. Add the crushed ginger slices and bring to a boil. Add the clams and cover. Reduce to a simmer and cook 4 minutes, or until the clams open.

3] Meanwhile combine the black beans, garlic, and minced ginger in a small bowl. Combine the sauce ingredients in a bowl. Mix 2 tablespoons of the sauce with the black bean mixture to moisten. Place the cornstarch in another small bowl.

4] With a bamboo strainer or slotted spoon, transfer the opened clams to a bowl, cover with a towel, and set aside. Combine the reserved clam cooking liquid with the cornstarch for thickening.

5] Place a wok over high heat. Swirl in the peanut oil and stir-fry the black bean mixture 20 seconds. Pour in the sauce and the clams and stir-fry to combine and coat the shells, about 1 minute. With the sauce at a boil, make a well in the center and stir in the cornstarch mixture for an additional 30 seconds. Serve in bowls to catch the sauce.

RICE AND NOODLES

Just as rice is the focus of the meal in southern China, wheat-based products like noodles and dumplings are the focus in the north. Because of their importance in the Chinese diet, both of these simple starches are highly celebrated in culinary lore: Noodles symbolize longevity and are traditionally served at birthday celebrations. Legend has it that the longer the noodle, the longer the life of the eater.

In Chinese folklore, to eat rice too noisily, or greedily, is to chase away prosperity, while to leave some uneaten is a grievous insult to the host. Chinese children are taught that if they do leave rice in their bowls, their future spouse will be pock-marked. And a good child is, by definition, a good eater of rice.

BASIC WHITE RICE

The Chinese do not add salt or other seasonings to rice, since it is meant to accompany a wide range of carefully sauced foods. Rinsing removes excess surface starch so the cooked rice is fluffier and cleaner tasting, but it is not absolutely necessary. *Makes 3 cups cooked rice*

1 cup long-grain rice
2 cups water

1] Working in the sink, place the rice in a large mixing bowl and fill with cold water. Swirl around and then, holding the rice back with one hand, pour out the cloudy water. Repeat this procedure several times until the water runs clear.

2] Place the rice and 2 cups water in a medium heavy saucepan. Bring to a boil, cover, and reduce to a simmer. Cook 18 minutes. Let sit 10 minutes, fluff with a fork, and serve.

BARBECUED PORK
AND SHRIMP FRIED RICE

$\blacksquare$

In China, fried rice is eaten as an afternoon snack rather than as part of a meal. It is colored pale gold from just a dash of soy sauce. Consider this recipe a model for your own variations. Fried rice is easiest to make with day-old, cold rice. ✖ *Serves 4*

4 tablespoons peanut oil
½ pound medium shrimp, shelled
   and deveined
2 eggs, beaten with 1 teaspoon
   sesame oil and ½ teaspoon salt
3 scallions, white and green, sliced

3 cups cold cooked white rice
½ pound barbecued pork, cut in
   ½-inch cubes
2 teaspoons soy sauce
Dash white pepper

1] Heat the wok over high heat and swirl in 2 tablespoons of the peanut oil. Shake off any excess liquid from the shrimp to avoid splattering. Stir-fry shrimp just until pink, about 2 minutes, and tip out onto a platter, leaving about a tablespoon of oil in the pan.

2] Swirl in the eggs beaten with sesame oil and salt. Scramble until set but still runny. Tip off onto the platter and with a spoon break the egg into bite-sized pieces. Wipe the wok clean with paper towels and return to high heat.

3] Pour in the remaining 2 tablespoons of oil. Stir-fry the scallions for 20 seconds and then add the cold rice. Quickly spread it all over the pan, breaking up and loosening the grains while stir-frying. Add the barbecued pork, cooked shrimp, egg, soy sauce, and white pepper. Stir-fry to combine and heat through, 1 or 2 minutes, and serve.

VARIATIONS. Honey-cured ham, cut in ¼-inch slices and then diced, may be substituted for barbecued pork. Stir-fry diced carrots, peas, and reconstituted dried mushrooms for vegetable fried rice. Half a skinless, boneless chicken breast, cut in small cubes and seasoned with salt and pepper, can also be substituted for the shrimp. This is a dish of endless variations.

STEAMED RICE WITH CHINESE SAUSAGE AND DRIED SHRIMP

The strong flavors of sweet Chinese sausage and salty dried shrimp are balanced by steamed rice in this casual one-dish meal from cooking companion Betty Lew of Silver Lake, California. Serve with a plate of Broccoli with Oyster Sauce and Sesame Oil (see page 100) or Stir-fried Bok Choy with Garlic (see page 99) for an easy week-night supper.
Serves 6

3 large dried Chinese black mushrooms	4 cups water
	¼ cup dried shrimp
2 Chinese sweet sausages or lop cheung	3 scallions, white and green, thinly sliced
2 cups long-grain rice	Soy sauce

1] Soak the mushrooms in hot water for 15 minutes to soften, then drain. Trim tough stems and thinly slice the caps. Thinly slice the sausages along the diagonal.

2] Rinse the rice as for Basic White Rice (see page 83). Place in a medium saucepan with lid or an electric rice cooker. Pour in the water and bring to a boil, uncovered. After the water has boiled 2 minutes, stir in the mushrooms and dried shrimp. Top with sausage slices. Cover and cook at a low simmer for 18 minutes. Let sit, covered, 10 minutes. Fluff with a fork, scatter on the scallions, and serve with soy sauce.

ROAST PORK LO MEIN

Lo mein, or stir-fried noodles, tastes better cooked at home where you can use the freshest ingredients and control the amount of sugar and salt that goes into the sauce. Use this as a master recipe for your own favorite additions: slivered roasted duck, ham, or chicken are a few suggestions. ✕ *Serves 4*

½ pound dry Chinese egg noodles
   or spaghettini
4 tablespoons peanut oil
½ pound barbecued pork, thinly
   sliced
3 scallions, white and green
1 large cucumber, peeled
½ pound (about 1 cup) bean
   sprouts

SAUCE

2 tablespoons soy sauce
2 tablespoons oyster sauce
1 tablespoon dry sherry
1 teaspoon sesame oil
½ teaspoon salt
½ teaspoon sugar

1 tablespoon minced garlic
1 tablespoon minced fresh ginger

1] Bring a large pot of salted water to a boil. Cook the noodles, stirring frequently to separate the strands, until just done, 3 to 4 minutes. Drain in a colander and rinse with cold water, separating the strands with your fingers to cool evenly. Transfer to a large bowl and toss with 1 tablespoon of the peanut oil. Noodles may be prepared up to 4 hours in advance and kept, covered, in the refrigerator.

2] Meanwhile slice the meat and vegetables into thin strips. (Lo mein is such a quick-cooking dish that you want to have everything chopped and nearby once you start stir-frying.) Cut the pork slices into matchsticks about 1 inch long by ⅛ inch thick. Cut the scallions into 2-inch lengths and then slice thinly lengthwise. Cut the cucumber into 2-inch lengths and then in half lengthwise. Remove the seeds, thinly slice, and then julienne. Arrange the meat and vegetables on a platter, along with the bean sprouts, for easy access near the stove.

3] Combine the sauce ingredients in a bowl.

4] Heat a wok or large skillet over high heat. Heat the remaining 3 tablespoons of peanut oil and then stir-fry the garlic and ginger just until their aroma is released. Stir-fry the pork and scallions briefly and then add the cucumber and bean sprouts for a total of 1 minute. Pour in the sauce, toss well and add the cooked noodles. Stir-fry to combine all the ingredients and heat the noodles through, about 1 minute more. Tip out onto a serving platter and serve hot or at room temperature.

Summer Noodles with Spicy Peanut Sauce

Chinese sesame paste can be substituted for peanut butter, if you prefer your noodles sesame-flavored. *Serves 4*

½ pound dry Chinese egg noodles or spaghettini
1 tablespoon sesame oil

Sauce

2 garlic cloves, peeled and crushed
¼-inch length fresh ginger, peeled and crushed
2 tablespoons soy sauce
¼ cup smooth peanut butter, or sesame paste
1 tablespoon sesame oil
2 tablespoons rice vinegar
2 tablespoons chicken stock
2 teaspoons chili oil
1 tablespoon sugar

2 cucumbers, peeled, seeded, and shredded, for garnish
¼ cup chopped fresh cilantro, for garnish

1] Bring a large saucepan or stockpot of water to a boil. Cook the noodles, stirring occasionally, until al dente, about 3 minutes. Drain and rinse thoroughly with cold water. Transfer to a serving bowl and toss with the tablespoon of sesame oil. Reserve at room temperature.

2] Mince the garlic and ginger in a blender or food processor. Then add all of the remaining sauce ingredients and purée until smooth. Transfer to a bowl and reserve at room temperature if making in advance.

3] To serve, toss noodles with peanut sauce. Sprinkle with cucumbers and cilantro.

NOODLES WITH PEKING MEAT SAUCE

Similar in concept to an Italian meat sauce, this fragrant, spicy pork topping is a favorite northern Chinese street food. The sauce can be made in advance and reheated for smaller portions and snacks.

✗ *Serves 4*

SAUCE
1 cup Chinese Chicken Stock (see page 23)
2 tablespoons ground bean sauce
¼ cup hoisin sauce
¼ cup dry sherry
1 tablespoon Chinese black vinegar
1 teaspoon Chinese chili sauce
1 cinnamon stick

2 tablespoons peanut oil
2 tablespoons minced garlic

1 tablespoon minced fresh ginger
¾ pound ground pork

12 ounces Chinese egg noodles or spaghettini
1 tablespoon sesame oil
1 cucumber, peeled, seeded, and thinly cut in strips, for garnish
4 scallions, thinly sliced, for garnish
½ bunch cilantro for garnish

1] Measure out and combine all the sauce ingredients in a bowl.

2] Heat the peanut oil in a wok or large skillet over high heat. Stir-fry the garlic and ginger until their aroma is released, 30 seconds. Add the pork, stirring to break up the meat and brown evenly, about 5 minutes.

3] Pour in the sauce mixture and bring to a boil. Skim and discard any foam that rises to the top. Reduce to a simmer and cook, uncovered, until most of the moisture has evaporated, about 25 minutes. Remove the cinnamon stick. The completed sauce can now be kept in the refrigerator for 2 to 3 days and reheated as needed.

4] To make the noodles, bring a large stockpot of salted water to a boil over high heat. Cook the noodles, stirring occasionally, until al dente. Chinese noodles cook more quickly than Italian, so start testing after about 3 minutes. Drain in a colander and transfer to a serving bowl. Immediately toss with the tablespoon of sesame oil to coat. Top with the warm meat sauce, but do not toss as you would Italian pasta.

5] Arrange bowls of cucumbers, scallions, and cilantro on the table. Serve portions of the noodles topped with sauce for guests to garnish to taste.

CRISP NOODLE PANCAKE ("TWO-SIDES BROWN")

Shallow-fried noodles develop a crisp brown crust that is the perfect foil for stir-fry dishes with rich gravies. The only trick to making crisp, savory noodle pancakes is to leave enough time for the boiled noodles to cool and dry before frying. *Serves 4 as an accompaniment*

½ pound dried Chinese egg noodles or spaghettini

4 tablespoons peanut oil
Salt

1] Bring a large pot of water to a boil. Cook the noodles, stirring occasionally, until al dente, 4 to 5 minutes. Drain in a colander and rinse well with cold water, fluffing the strands to separate.

2] When the noodles are thoroughly cool, lift them, shaking off excess water, and place in an even layer on a dinner plate or platter. Set aside at room temperature, uncovered, at least 1 hour or up to 4 hours to dry. If preparing a day in advance, after the noodles have air-dried, cover with plastic wrap and refrigerate.

3] To fry the pancake, heat a cast-iron or other large, heavy skillet over high heat. When the pan is hot, pour in 2 tablespoons of the peanut oil. Transfer the noodles to the pan in an even layer. Fry over high heat until crisp and brown on the bottom, about 5 minutes. (Do not worry about a few blackened spots. They add authenticity.) Lift with a spatula, holding the top with the palm of your hand or another utensil, and flip over. Drizzle in the remaining peanut oil along the edges, lifting the pancake to distribute the oil. Fry until the bottom is brown and crisp. Transfer to a serving platter, season with salt, and top with a moist stir-fry dish such as Bok Choy Beef (see page 62) or Chicken Chow Mein (see page 91).

TOSSED SEAFOOD
CHOW MEIN

●

This light seafood and noodle dish is a nice change from the Italian pasta dishes you may be more familiar with. It makes a substantial casual dinner when accompanied by a simple green like Long Beans with Garlic and Chiles (page 96) or Broccoli with Oyster Sauce and Sesame Oil (page 100). ✖ *Serves 2 to 4*

½ pound Chinese dried noodles or
   spaghettini

SAUCE
⅔ cup chicken stock
2 tablespoons light soy sauce
2 tablespoons lemon juice
1 teaspoon sesame oil
½ teaspoon salt
¼ teaspoon white pepper
¼ teaspoon sugar

½ pound medium shrimp, shelled
   and deveined
½ pound bay scallops
2 teaspoons minced garlic
1 teaspoon minced fresh ginger
6 ounces bok choy (about 2 large
   stalks), roughly chopped
7 tablespoons peanut oil

1] Bring a large saucepan or stockpot of water to a boil. Cook the noodles at a rapid boil until done, 3 to 5 minutes. Drain in a colander and rinse in cold water, fluffing the strands to separate and cool evenly. Shake off excess water and place on a dinner plate or platter to air-dry for a minimum of 1 hour. Noodles can be covered with plastic wrap and reserved in the refrigerator for a day.

2] Mix the sauce ingredients together in a bowl. Rinse the seafood with cold water and pat dry with paper towels. Prepare garlic, ginger, and bok choy.

3] Place the wok over high heat. Swirl in 2 tablespoons of the peanut oil. Stir-fry the shrimp for 30 seconds. Add the scallops and continue stir-frying until they are just opaque, about 1 minute. Tip out into a bowl, along with any pan juices, and reserve.

4] Return the wok to high heat. Swirl in 4 tablespoons of the oil and fry the noodles until brown and crisp, about 3 minutes. Transfer to a platter, scraping vigorously with a spoon to remove any noodles.

5] Return wok to high heat and swirl in the remaining tablespoon of oil. Stir-fry the garlic and ginger 10 seconds and then add the bok choy. Stir-fry an additional 30 seconds.

6] Return the pan-fried noodles and cooked seafood with juices to the pan. Pour in the sauce. Vigorously stir-fry, using 2 spoons if necessary, breaking and tossing the noodles to combine well, for about 2 minutes. Serve hot.

CHICKEN CHOW MEIN

Chow mein is essentially boiled noodles, which are then shallow-fried and combined with sliced vegetables or meat and a sauce.
✖ *Serves 4*

½ pound skinless, boneless
   chicken breast, cubed

MARINADE_____
½ egg white
½ teaspoon salt
¼ teaspoon white pepper

_____

1 cup broccoli florets
1 small carrot, peeled, cut in half
   lengthwise, and sliced
2 bok choy stalks, cut in half
   lengthwise and sliced
4 ounces mushrooms, quartered

SAUCE_____
¾ cup chicken stock
1 tablespoon oyster sauce
1 teaspoon soy sauce
¼ teaspoon black pepper

_____

2 tablespoons cornstarch mixed
   with 2 tablespoons water
1 recipe Crisp Noodle Pancake
   (see page 89)
4 tablespoons peanut oil
1 tablespoon minced garlic

1] Combine the cubed chicken with the marinade in a mixing bowl. Reserve in the refrigerator. Then cut all the vegetables and arrange near the stove. Combine the sauce ingredients in a small bowl. Make the cornstarch mixture and set aside.

2] Fry the noodle pancake in 2 tablespoons of oil, place on a platter, and reserve in a 200 F oven.

3] Heat the wok over high heat. Swirl in 2 tablespoons of oil and stir-fry the chicken just until opaque, about 1 minute. Tip the chicken onto a plate and swirl the remaining oil into the pan.

4] Stir-fry the garlic 20 seconds. Then add the broccoli and carrot and stir-fry a minute. Add the bok choy and mushrooms and briefly stir-fry. Pour in the sauce and return the chicken to the pan. Stir and toss until the mixture is well combined.

5] With the heat still high, drizzle in the cornstarch mixture, stirring constantly to thicken and coat the pieces. Place over the crisp noodle pancake and serve.

ANTS CLIMBING A TREE

In this satisfying homestyle dish from Szechuan, dried mung bean threads and ground pork absorb and carry a harmonious blend of rich, savory flavors. ✖ *Serves 4*

4 ounces bean threads

SAUCE_____
¾ cup chicken stock
1½ tablespoons soy sauce
2 teaspoons ground bean sauce
1 teaspoon sugar
½ teaspoon sesame oil
½ teaspoon Chinese chili sauce
_____

2 tablespoons minced garlic
3 tablespoons chopped scallions,
  white and green
1 tablespoon minced fresh ginger
1 tablespoon peanut oil
½ pound ground pork
½ teaspoon salt
⅓ cup fresh chopped cilantro, for
  garnish (optional)

1] Soak the bean threads in a large bowl of hot water for 15 minutes to soften. Lift out, shaking off any excess water, and then cut in half with a knife.

2] Meanwhile combine the sauce ingredients in a bowl. Chop all of the seasonings and have ready near the stove.

3] Heat the wok over high heat. Swirl in the peanut oil and stir-fry the garlic, scallions, and ginger for 30 seconds. Add the pork and salt and stir-fry, breaking up the meat with a spoon so it browns evenly.

4] When the pinkness is gone, pour in the sauce and the bean threads. Reduce to a simmer and cook, uncovered, until the liquid is nearly all absorbed, about 5 minutes. Transfer to a serving bowl, sprinkle with cilantro if desired, and serve hot.

VEGETABLE SIDE DISHES

SIMPLE VEGETABLE COOKERY IS SO ESTEEMED IN CHINA THAT THERE IS A WORD TO DESCRIBE THE PERFECTLY CRUNCHY, QUICK-COOKED VEGETABLE'S TASTE—*HSEIN*. IT IS WORTH A TRIP TO A CHINESE MARKET TO GLIMPSE THE WONDERFUL ARRAY OF FRESH GREENS AVAILABLE. DON'T BE AFRAID TO EXPERIMENT. MOST NEED ONLY BE BRIEFLY STIR-FRIED AND PERHAPS BRAISED IN A BIT OF CHICKEN STOCK FOR EXCELLENT RESULTS.

COLD TOSSED ASPARAGUS WITH SESAME SEEDS

While there is no tradition of salad in China, there is a large repertoire of pickled vegetables and cold dishes such as this for refreshing the palate. ✂ *Serves 6*

1 pound asparagus	1 teaspoon rice vinegar
2 teaspoons sesame seeds	1 teaspoon light soy sauce
1½ tablespoons peanut oil	¼ teaspoon sugar
2 teaspoons sesame oil	

1] Snap off and discard the tough ends of asparagus. Cut stalks into 1-inch lengths on the diagonal. Bring a medium saucepan of salted water to a boil. Add the asparagus and cook until tender-crisp, about 3 minutes. Drain in a colander and then immediately rinse with cold water to cool. Pat dry with paper towels.

2] Place the sesame seeds in a small skillet and toast over medium-low heat, tossing occasionally, until golden, about 5 minutes. Reserve.

3] Stir the remaining ingredients together in a small bowl. Place the asparagus in a shallow ceramic serving dish, pour on the seasoning mixture, and toss with a spoon. Sprinkle with sesame seeds and toss again. Cover with plastic wrap and chill at least 2 hours. Serve cold or at room temperature.

VARIATION. Raw cucumbers (about 1 pound), peeled, quartered lengthwise, seeded, and then cut in ½-inch lengths, can be substituted for asparagus.

Long Beans with
Garlic and Chiles

As with all chile dishes, adjust the number to taste. ✖ *Serves 4*

12 ounces Chinese long beans or
  green beans
1½ tablespoons peanut oil
3 large garlic cloves, peeled and
  slivered

1 teaspoon coarse salt
3 dried red chiles, cut in ¼-inch
  lengths
⅓ cup chicken stock

1] Trim the beans and cut Chinese long beans into 2-inch lengths or green beans into 1-inch lengths.

2] Heat the oil in a large skillet or wok over high heat. Sir-fry the garlic for just a second and then add the beans and salt. Stir-fry about a minute, just to coat the beans.

3] Scatter in the red chiles, pour in the stock, and cook, uncovered, until the liquid is nearly evaporated, about 10 minutes. Just a light glaze should remain on the beans. Serve hot or at room temperature.

Snow Peas and Water
Chestnuts

A delicious and classic combination; you can make this in no time. ✖ *Serves 6*

¾ pound Chinese snow peas or
  sugar snap peas
5 water chestnuts, washed and
  peeled
2 tablespoons peanut oil

1 teaspoon salt
1½ tablespoons minced fresh
  ginger
2 teaspoons sesame oil

1] Trim the tough ends of the peapods. (String sugar snaps if you use them.) Slice the water chestnuts into thin circles.

2] Heat the peanut oil over high heat in a wok or large skillet. Stir-fry the peas and water chestnuts with salt until they begin to soften, about 2 minutes. Add the ginger and sesame oil, cook an additional minute, and serve.

Chinese Cooking for Beginners

SZECHUAN EGGPLANT

Eggplant is a great sponge for the sweet, salty, spicy flavors of Szechuan. This is substantial enough to serve as a vegetarian main course. *Serves 6*

1½ pounds Japanese eggplant, washed and trimmed
1 tablespoon ground bean paste
2 tablespoons soy sauce
2 tablespoons dry sherry
2 tablespoons Chinese black vinegar
2 tablespoons sugar
½ teaspoon Szechuan peppercorns, roasted and ground (see page 16)

½ teaspoon chili oil
1 teaspoon sesame oil
1 teaspoon cornstarch mixed with 2 teaspoons water
¼ cup peanut oil
¼ cup minced garlic
1 tablespoon minced fresh ginger

1] Cut the eggplant into ¼-inch slices on the diagonal. (It is not necessary to salt or peel Asian eggplants.) Transfer to a bowl near the stove.

2] Combine the bean paste, soy sauce, sherry, vinegar, sugar, peppercorns, chili oil, and sesame oil in a small bowl. Have the cornstarch and water mixture ready nearby.

3] Heat the peanut oil in a wok over medium-high heat. Stir-fry the garlic and ginger briefly, being careful not to brown the garlic.

4] Add the eggplant, turn up the heat, and stir-fry until the eggplant is lightly golden, about 5 minutes.

5] Pour in the soy sauce mixture and stir to evenly coat the eggplant. Cover, reduce the heat to medium-low, and cook 3 minutes.

6] Uncover and turn up the heat. Pour in the cornstarch mixture, stirring constantly to thicken. Toss to combine and serve hot.

Chinese Cooking for Beginners

STIR-FRIED BOK CHOY
WITH GARLIC

Bok choy, now available in most supermarkets, has a tart, astringent quality similar to spinach. I love it cooked simply, so its fresh taste shines through. ✖ *Serves 6*

1½ pounds bok choy
1½ tablespoons peanut oil
4 garlic cloves, peeled, crushed,
　　and cut in thin slivers

1 teaspoon salt

1] Separate the stalks of bok choy. Wash and pat dry. Cut each stalk in half lengthwise and then chop into 2-inch lengths. Transfer to a bowl or platter.

2] Heat a wok or large skillet over medium-high heat. Swirl in the peanut oil and add the garlic. Stir-fry for a few seconds, being careful not to brown. Add the bok choy and salt and turn the heat to high. Stir-fry until leaves are wilted and bright green but stalks are still crunchy, about 3 minutes. Tip onto a platter and serve hot.

STIR-FRIED BEAN SPROUTS

In China, bean sprouts are known as vegetables for the teeth, for their crisp texture. It is not necessary to wash bean sprouts, since they are grown indoors, in water, not soil. Washing will only make them soggy. ✖ *Serves 6*

1 tablespoon peanut oil
6 scallions, white and green parts,
　　cut in ½-inch lengths on the
　　diagonal
1 pound bean sprouts

1½ teaspoons salt
2 tablespoons chicken stock
2 teaspoons sesame oil

1] Heat the oil in a wok or large skillet over high heat. Stir-fry the scallions about 20 seconds. Then add the bean sprouts and salt. Stir and toss 30 seconds more.

2] Pour in the chicken stock and stir-fry about 1½ minutes. Drizzle with sesame oil and serve hot.

BROCCOLI WITH OYSTER SAUCE AND SESAME OIL

Chinese broccoli, available at specialty markets, is long-stemmed and leafy, with a more acidic, fuller flavor than ordinary broccoli. It is one of the world's most nutritious vegetables—high in calcium and in vitamins A and C. Cooked with oyster sauce and sesame oil, it matches well with almost any Chinese menu. Italian broccoli rabe or American-style broccoli may be substituted. ✖ *Serves 4 to 6*

1 pound broccoli (Chinese if possible), bottom 2 inches of stems trimmed
Salt
2 tablespoons oyster sauce
1 tablespoon dry sherry

2 tablespoons water
2 teaspoons sesame oil
½ teaspoon sugar
1 tablespoon cornstarch mixed with 1 tablespoon water
1 tablespoon peanut oil

1] Cut the broccoli into long, thin florets. Fill a large saucepan with about 4 inches of water and bring to a boil. Add a large pinch of salt and blanch the broccoli for 1 minute once the water returns to a boil. Drain and rinse with cold water.

2] In a small bowl combine the oyster sauce, dry sherry, water, sesame oil, and sugar. Also prepare the cornstarch mixture.

3] Heat a dry wok over high heat. Swirl in the peanut oil and then stir-fry the broccoli for 5 seconds, just to coat with oil. Pour in the sauce mixture and stir and toss an additional minute. With the sauce at a boil, drizzle in the cornstarch mixture, stirring constantly until sauce thickens and coats the broccoli, less than a minute. Serve hot.

Chinese Cooking for Beginners

DESSERTS

THESE EASY DESSERTS RESPOND TO THE AMERICAN TASTE for something sensational and sweet at the end of the meal. For every day, however, nothing beats fresh sliced oranges or other seasonal fruits after a Chinese meal.

WARM BANANAS WITH GINGER AND COCONUT

New cooks are understandably anxious about flambéing. Sure it sounds like fun, but what if the kitchen catches on fire or the smoke alarm goes berserk? Not to worry. These foolproof, step-by-step directions are guaranteed to work.

The purpose of flambéing is to burn off the alcohol so only the taste remains, so don't be afraid to let the flames burn. They will eventually go out. While this dessert is certainly rich enough alone, it is also delicious served alongside vanilla ice cream. ✖ *Serves 4*

¾ cup shredded, unsweetened coconut

4 tablespoons (½ stick) unsalted butter

1 tablespoon minced fresh ginger

4 large, firm bananas, peeled

¼ cup brown sugar

¼ cup orange liqueur such as triple sec or Grand Marnier

2 tablespoons fresh lemon juice

1] Toast the coconut in a dry 10-inch skillet over medium heat until golden, about 2 minutes. Coconut is easily burned so stay nearby and stir often to avoid scorching. Transfer to a bowl and wipe the skillet clean with paper towels.

2] Return the skillet to medium-high heat and melt the butter. Sauté the ginger about 1 minute. Then add the whole bananas and brown sugar. Cook, turning the bananas to distribute and dissolve the sugar, about 2 minutes. Using tongs, transfer bananas to individual dessert plates or a platter.

3] Turn the heat up to high. Pour in the orange liqueur and light a match. Touch the surface of the sauce with the match just until it ignites. Then put out the match and continue cooking the sauce until the flames subside. Turn off the heat and swirl in the lemon juice.

4] Pour the warm sauce over the bananas. Sprinkle with toasted coconut and serve warm.

CHOCOLATE-DIPPED FORTUNE COOKIES

Los Angeles, the city that gave the world smog, right turns on red lights, and kosher burritos, also gave birth to Chinese fortune cookies. They were invented at a local Cantonese noodle factory and were eventually introduced to China by Chinese-Americans returning home. These chocolate-covered fortune cookies are great fun to serve at parties.
✖ *Makes about 40 cookies*

Two 4.5-ounce boxes Chinese
 fortune cookies (40 cookies)

6 ounces good quality bittersweet
 or semisweet chocolate

1] Unwrap the cookies and have ready nearby.

2] To melt the chocolate, make a double boiler by bringing about an inch of water to a simmer in a saucepan in which a mixing bowl can nestle without touching the water. Have ready a baking tray or platter lined with parchment paper or aluminum foil. Roughly chop the chocolate. Place in the mixing bowl over the pan of simmering water and stir with a spatula until melted and smooth. Remove from heat.

3] Pick up each cookie at one tip, and with the spatula generously coat the half you are not holding. Place sideways on the lined baking tray, leaving space between the cookies. Refrigerate, uncovered, until the chocolate hardens, about 2 hours. These taste best if refrigerated until serving time. They will keep at room temperature after the chocolate has hardened; however, they will eventually lose their crispness.

TANGERINE SHERBET

Chinese markets sell tangerines with the leaves and stems still on. The green leaves make a beautiful garnish for this fresh, cool dessert.

✖ *Serves 4 to 6*

Grated zest of 2 tangerines
1 cup sugar
1 cup water

1½ cups tangerine juice, strained
½ cup fresh lemon juice

1] Combine the grated tangerine zest, sugar, and water in a heavy saucepan. Bring to a boil, stirring occasionally, until the sugar is dissolved and a syrup has formed, about 5 minutes. Set aside to cool 10 minutes and then strain.

2] In a medium mixing bowl, combine the strained sugar syrup with tangerine and lemon juices. Cover and chill 2 hours.

3] Pour into an ice cream maker and follow instructions for sorbet or sherbet. The finished sherbet can be stored in a plastic container in the freezer for a week.

POACHED PEARS IN
HONEY GINGER SYRUP

This easy light dessert was inspired by Chinese chef and cookbook author Kenneth Lo. Make it a day in advance and serve with a winter menu. ✖ *Serves 4*

4 firm, ripe pears such as Anjou	2 teaspoons minced fresh ginger
Approximately 5 cups water	1 cinnamon stick
¼ cup plus 2 tablespoons honey	Juice of ½ lemon

1] With a sharp paring knife or serrated blade, carefully peel the pears, leaving the stems on.

2] Pour water into a heavy medium saucepan. Add the honey, ginger, and cinnamon and bring to a boil, stirring occasionally to dissolve the honey. Reduce to a simmer and then add the pears. If the pears are not covered, add water to cover. Simmer about 45 minutes, or until the water is reduced by half.

3] With a slotted spoon transfer the pears to a ceramic bowl or roasting pan and set aside.

4] Turn up the heat on the syrup and boil about 10 minutes, until reduced again by half. Strain the liquid and stir in the lemon juice. Set aside until it cools to room temperature. Then pour syrup over the pears and cover with plastic wrap. Chill at least 4 hours or as long as 48. Serve cold.

BOOKS ON CHINESE CUISINE AND CULTURE

Anderson, E. N. *The Food of China*. Yale University Press, New Haven, 1988.

This impassioned anthropologist traces the history of food in China from prehistoric Peking man to modern Hong Kong Chinese. For a thorough understanding of the regional differences and origin of Chinese food rituals, with entertaining anecdotes, this is the book food writers refer to.

Carpenter, Hugh. *Pacific Flavors*. Stewart, Tabori & Chang, New York, 1988.

————. *Chopstix*. Stewart, Tabori & Chang, New York, 1990.

Hugh Carpenter's beautifully photographed books capture the sun-swept California life we can all dream of. The recipes are easy-to-follow, clear representations of this popular cooking teacher's exuberant East/West style.

Cost, Bruce. *Bruce Cost's Asian Ingredients*. William Morrow, New York, 1988.

Cost, a highly regarded Chinese food scholar, chef, writer, and restaurateur, is *the* authority on Asian foodstuffs. Much more than a list of ingredients, this practical book includes entertaining information on the origin and folklore of esoteric ingredients as well as advice on purchasing, storing, recommended brands, and identifying photos. It also contains a collection of highly original, accessible recipes.

Hom, Ken. *Ken Hom's Chinese Cookery*. Harper & Row, New York, 1986.

————. *East Meets West*. Simon & Schuster, New York, 1987.

————. *Fragrant Harbor Taste*. Simon & Schuster, New York, 1989.

————. *The Taste of China*. Simon & Schuster, New York, 1990.

Chinese-American chef and author Ken Hom is the premiere popularizer of Chinese cooking in America. His books are all invitingly designed and clearly written with an understanding of how Americans wish to prepare Chinese food at home—without too much oil, fuss, or bother. His coffee-table picture book, *The Taste of China*, researched during the student uprisings of 1989, stands alone. Unlike most food picture books that prettify their subjects, his is an honest portrayal in words and pictures of the communal kitchens, street vendors, state restaurants, and primitive home kitchens producing Chinese cuisine today. The rustic homestyle recipes sound luscious.

Kuo, Irene. *The Key to Chinese Cooking.* Alfred A. Knopf, New York, 1977.

When restaurateur Kuo produced her masterwork in 1977 she was touted as the Julia Child of Chinese cooking because her knowledge was so thorough and her technique so clear. Though she may not have succeeded in as large a way as Child did, her recipes remain foolproof and delicious.

Leung, Mai. *The Classic Chinese Cookbook.* Harper & Row, New York, 1976.

I have a special affection for this, my first Chinese cookbook. The author's friendly commentary and clear recipe-writing style carry the reader through the complete repertoire of classic Chinese cuisine without a hitch.

Lin, Hsiang Ju & Tsuifeng. *Chinese Gastronomy.* Perigee, New York, 1982.

These enthusiastic authors researched ancient cookbooks as well as the works of philosophers and poets to elucidate the principles of Chinese flavor and texture for a foreign audience. Though recipes for sea slug, jelly fish, and tripe may be a bit too authentic for most American tastes, their philosophy lays the groundwork for a clear understanding of the workings of the Chinese kitchen.

Tropp, Barbara. *The Modern Art of Chinese Cooking.* William Morrow, New York, 1982.

If you can never know too much about what you are eating and how to cook it, Tropp's passionate and densely packed text is for you. The author, who was a graduate student of Chinese literature and history and lived in Taiwan for two years before becoming a chef and restaurateur, brings her unremitting energy to bear on the philosophy, culture, and culinary lore surrounding the entire repertoire of classic Chinese recipes.

Yan, Martin. *The Yan Can Cook Book.* Doubleday, New York, 1981.
————. *A Wok For All Seasons.* Doubleday, New York, 1988.
While many cooking authorities preach the fun and ease of food prep-

aration, ebullient television chef Martin Yan practices it. His practical recipe collections are pared-down renditions of traditional restaurant dishes truly made quick and easy.

Zee, A. *Swallowing Clouds*. Simon & Schuster, New York, 1990.

In this charmingly eccentric book, the author uses the characters on a Chinese restaurant menu to illustrate the connection between the Chinese love of food, the culture surrounding it, and its effect on the development of language. Although a few simple recipes are included, the book's main purpose is to entertain and inspire. A wonderful gift for your favorite Chinese restaurant aficionado.

INDEX

Index